Blood of the Lamb

Saints, Sinners and Slavery

Blood of the Lamb

Saints, Sinners and Slavery

Dorothy Butters

First published in the UK in 2024 by Shakspeare Editorial, UK

Copyright © 2024 Dorothy Butters

ISBN 978-1-0685716-0-2 (paperback)
ISBN 978-1-0685716-1-9 (ebook)

All rights reserved. No part of this publication may be reproduced or used in any manner without written permission from the publisher.

No part of this book may be used or reproduced in any manner for the purpose of training artificial intelligence technologies or systems.

The moral rights of the author have been asserted.

Design www.ShakspeareEditorial.org

All photographs copyright of the author

This book is dedicated to Harry Potter, who inspired me to volunteer in prisons, encouraged me to write this book, and has been a dear and steadfast friend for fifty years.

Contents

Prologue	1
Introduction	3

PART ONE

1. The Tobacco Lords	7
2. Richard of Auchincruive: A tree bearing fruits of good and evil	25
3. George Oswald of Scotstoun and His Heirs	50
Richard Alexander Oswald	52
James Oswald	55
Alexander Haldane Oswald	57
The Haldanes	60
4. The Reformation and the Evangelicals	61
Elizabeth Oswald	67
5. The Haldanes: Authoritarian Evangelicals or Liberals?	69
6. The Oswalds in Scotstoun	84
Part Two	97
7. The Brethren	99
8. Anniesland Mansions	112
9. The Jacksons	121
Nessie	140
10. Fellowship	148
11. Service	167
12. Going Into All the World to Preach the Gospel	177
13. The Winds of Change	192
Postscript	210
Acknowledgements	214
Bibliography	216
Family Trees	219
Index	224

Illustrations

1. The gallery in Auchincruive church with, at the end, Richard's armchair	49
2. Anniesland in 1936 showing a Gospel Tent	120
3. Anniesland Hall	120
4. Jack and Willie	147
5. Jack and Nessie's wedding	147
6. Jack and his pupils	176
Oswald family tree	220
Talbot Crosbie family tree	221
Alexander Oswald family tree	222
Haldane family tree	223

Abbreviations

BBC British Broadcasting Corporation – a public service broadcaster

CYC Christian Youth Centre

EULSC Edinburgh University Library Special Collections

GCSE General Certificate of Secondary Education

GUEA Glasgow United Evangelistic Association

MV motor vessel

POW prisoner of war

SCEM Scottish Counties Evangelistic Movement

SPGH Society for the Propagation of the Gospel at Home

UCS Upper Clyde Shipbuilders

Prologue

Every morning, my father Jack read a passage from the Bible to my mother, my brother and me. One day, when I was eight or nine, it was the story of Abraham and Isaac. God commanded the aged Abraham to take his only son Isaac, whom he loved, to a far-off place and sacrifice him as a burnt offering. Abraham got up early the next morning and took Isaac, a knife, wood and some fire to the place God had told him of. Abraham laid the wood on the altar and raised his knife to smite the boy. At the last minute, the angel of the Lord called out, ordering Abraham to stay his hand and sacrifice instead a ram which had been caught by its horns in a nearby thicket. Jack closed the bible, completed his usual prayer that the family live the coming day to God's glory, turned to my mother and sighed, 'I hope the Lord never asks me to make a sacrifice like that.'

I assessed my chances of survival. I reluctantly abandoned the hope that my mother might dissuade Jack from sacrificing me, as a wife was obliged, if push came to shove, to love, honour and obey; knowing that Jack doted on me was worse than useless – the more he loved me, the more God would insist that he slay me. After all, rather than repeat Cain's catastrophic error of skimping on his offering, Abraham had risen early the very next morning to satisfy his jealous God. I mulled this over as I went downstairs, out of the close, under Anniesland Hall's huge neon sign proclaiming 'Christ died for our sins' and headed for school.

Decades later I realised that I had overestimated my importance. God would have demanded the sacrifice of my older brother.

Introduction

Seeing the rise of fundamentalism in the Islamic world and political evangelicalism in the United States, I became curious about another fundamentalist movement – the Plymouth Brethren and, in particular, Anniesland Hall in Glasgow. My parents were committed members of this Hall and, growing up in the 1960s and early 1970s, I benefited from the all-embracing sense of home and belonging in a close-knit community. Although I left Scotland and the Brethren in 1974, when I was seventeen and chafing at the constrictions of the embrace, this community has continued to provide love, joy and support in my hours of need.

When I was growing up, Anniesland Hall was wealthy and vibrant, but by the late 1970s it struggled increasingly with the pressures of rapid change, until internal conflicts led to a schism in 1989.

Now, as ideologies and social norms continue to evolve, I want to understand the origins of Anniesland Hall and the world that formed it, complementing my subjective experiences with a fuller, properly researched understanding of the history leading to its creation and downfall. I followed the money and discovered that this Christian community not only owed its prominence to death and misery, to the scourge of slavery and the spoils of war, but also to ideals, hope and love.

This is the story of a city, and of a community and two families who formed and were formed by it. It is a story of wealth and spirituality, of certainty and doubt, of goodness and of the evil that good men can do. It starts in the late sixteenth century with a group of men known as the Tobacco Lords.

PART ONE

1. The Tobacco Lords

Honeymooning in Florence in 1878, James William Gordon Oswald asked his bride what she desired as a wedding gift. The young woman gazed up at the austere, geometric proportions of the Basilica di San Lorenzo, its classic lines a fresh and dignified relief from the overwrought Italian baroque churches, and replied, 'I would like you to build me a church in Anniesland like this one.' Oswald granted her wish and built a church – Anniesland Hall. Or so my mother told me.

The story is plausible.

Oswald's bride belonged to a devout Plymouth Brethren family and Oswald certainly had the means to fulfil his pledge. He had inherited land in Anniesland and vast family wealth which had been amassed by his forefathers in the seventeenth and eighteenth centuries when they traded in slaves, tobacco and war.

The Oswald family came originally from Kirkwall, in the bleak Orkney islands, thirty miles off the north coast of Scotland. James Oswald (c.1590–c.1660), had two sons, James and George, both of whom became ministers in Caithness, in the northeast of the Scottish mainland. Reflecting those disputatious times (see Chapter 3) James was an Episcopalian and George a Presbyterian.[1]

The Episcopalian James also had two sons – Richard, born in 1687 and Alexander, born in 1694 – who both moved south to Glasgow. They arrived in the right place at the right time for ambitious young men seeking their fortune, for that fortune would lie in the tobacco trade which was beginning to flourish in Glasgow. Through ambition, luck and judgement, Richard and Alexander became powerful members of a group of merchants known as the Tobacco Lords, who were major figures in the Atlantic trade and in the city of Glasgow itself.

Glasgow stands on the banks of the river Clyde, which rises in the Lanarkshire hills and flows through the Scottish industrial belt out to the Atlantic Ocean. The Clyde estuary, the Firth of Clyde, is a relatively sheltered waterway protected from the tumult of the Atlantic by the island of Arran, the Mull of Kintyre, and the Inner Hebrides. While the majesty of the highlands can be glimpsed in the snow-capped peaks on the horizon, there is a mellowness to the Firth of Clyde. The Gulf Stream warms the waters, keeping the land temperature mild enough for imported palm trees to flourish on the shores. Sailors voyaging homewards from the open seas are met on either side of the Firth by islands and gentle hills clad in gorse and heather, in subtle shades of blue and green or forming purple silhouettes against the sunset. From mediaeval

---

1. The Scottish Episcopalian church is governed by bishops, who are elected at a synod of clergy and laity. The Church of Scotland is Presbyterian and governed by elders.

1. The Tobacco Lords

times, smaller vessels could continue their voyage upstream past Gourock, where the river narrows and turns sharply east for a further fifteen miles to Glasgow, where the river crossing was overlooked by St Mungo's cathedral.

Although its cathedral is the oldest on the Scottish mainland and its university dates from 1451, until the seventeenth century Glasgow had been of minor importance in comparison with Scotland's capital, Edinburgh. However, by the 1630s Glasgow was becoming more assertive. It had developed new industries and the population of the city had almost doubled, from around 7,000 in the sixteenth century to about 12,000 in 1700. In those days Glasgow had no choice but to look to the west. To the north were hills, raiders and little money. To the south, trade with England was hampered by bad roads and protectionism in both kingdoms. Trade with Europe (mainly the Baltic, the Netherlands and France) was the preserve of the east coast ports, since any profits the Glasgow merchants could make there were eaten into by the heavy costs of a thirty-mile overland trip to Bo'ness on the Lothian coast, and fees to middlemen. As a result, Glasgow's maritime trade, apart from some exports of herring, hides and plaids to England and France, had been mainly with Argyll, the Inner Hebrides and Ireland.

When King James VI of Scotland became King James I of England in 1603 he hoped that the Union of the Crowns would also result in a political and economic union, but Glasgow's merchants had to wait for the Union of Parliaments in 1707 to participate legally in trade across the Atlantic. For decades they had enviously eyed England's flourishing commerce with its north American colonies, to which they had been granted only limited and sporadic official access. Long before 1707, unable to resist the lucrative trade in tobacco and sugar, the Glasgow merchants had established connections, and sometimes smuggling operations, with North America and the Caribbean. The first cargo of tobacco had arrived in Glasgow in 1674, although the goods were not landed directly in the city. The Clyde was barely navigable for the final fifteen miles to the city and larger ocean-going vessels had to transfer goods to shallow-draught boats at the estuary ports of Greenock, Wemyss Bay and Irvine. Consequently, in 1668, in anticipation of increased Atlantic trade, the City of Glasgow leased thirteen acres of land twenty miles down the Clyde where they built piers, quays, breakwaters and warehouses. This was the free port of Port Glasgow, which had its own Custom House to collect duties on the tobacco, sugar, rum, cotton and mahogany that was brought – legitimately or otherwise – from the Americas. Following the 1707 Acts of Union, Scottish merchants were finally granted the right to trade freely with the colonies and exploit the market for tobacco, sugar and slaves. They seized the opportunity. The stage was set for the triumph of the Tobacco Lords, among them the Oswald brothers.

According to McUre, who wrote a history of Glasgow in 1736,[2] Richard Oswald had been involved in 'sea adventures' before 1707, which gave

---

2. John McUre, *The History of Glasgow*.

him first-hand knowledge of the Caribbean and Virginia, personal contacts and access to commercial information. In 1713 he was appointed chief clerk in the Port Glasgow custom house, which put him in an ideal position to learn the details of duties pertaining, shipping routes and timetables, cargoes and onward freight. He and Alexander used this knowledge to expand their network and lay the foundations for the Oswalds' Atlantic business empire.

Geography gave the Glasgow merchants an advantage over tobacco traders elsewhere. The southwest coast of Scotland is precisely where the gulf stream carried ships from America several days earlier than to other British ports. Cargoes could be unloaded promptly and be the first to arrive on the European marketplace. The Tobacco Lords added to this geographical advantage by using a stores system they had developed while they were trading semi-legally in North America before 1707. Instead of using middlemen in a consignment system,[3] the Glasgow merchants employed a storekeeper, a trusted Scottish-born resident agent who would purchase tobacco direct from the growers, often in advance, so that the growers could buy such essentials as cloth, farming implements and leather goods from the company stores.

The Tobacco Lords owned their ships – forty-one in 1735,[4] when Glasgow's first 'foreign fleet'

---

3. Consignment is the act of consigning, or giving over goods to an agent's charge, custody or care but retaining legal ownership until the goods are sold. In terms of the accounts, these goods have neither been sold nor are part of the owner's inventory.
4. Daniel Defoe estimated that by 1725 Glasgow merchants were sending fifty ships a year to Virginia, New England and other colonies.

included the Oswald brothers' Martha, Amity and Speedwell – and sold the tobacco through their own agents in London and Europe. This, coupled with the stores system, facilitated a guaranteed cargo and a quicker turnaround for ships, and in theory allowed the storekeeper in America to quote the – mainly small – planters a better price. The storekeeper was often a relative, sometimes a son or nephew learning the trade – several of the great merchants had started out as assistant storekeepers – who could obtain valuable market intelligence to help the Tobacco Lords steal a march on the competition. The approach was so successful that in 1747 France granted Glasgow a monopoly to import tobacco to French territories. By the 1770s three quarters of the tobacco consumed in Europe was brought in by the Glasgow Tobacco Lords.

The men known as the Tobacco Lords, or Virginia Dons, were a tight-knit, exclusive group. Like the Oswalds, most did not come from wealthy or landed families, yet anyone embarking on a mercantile career in Glasgow needed a strong financial base from the outset. A man wishing to become a merchant had first to be a burgess or a member of a guild, which required a substantial down payment – long before any outlay on goods or shipping. The most reliable route to money was to inherit it or marry into it and, once the merchants had established themselves, they made sure that funds remained within their group and that they married as often as possible within the network. Neither Oswald brother married, but they had the support of their extended family – which included a

1. The Tobacco Lords

Moderator of the Church of Scotland[5] – and managed to join the Tobacco Lords.

There were other practical reasons for the Tobacco Lords' clannishness. Transatlantic trade was a precarious business in the eighteenth century. In addition to tempests, shipwrecks, crop failures and other vagaries of nature, pirates prowled the coasts and French warships frequently attacked British vessels on the high seas during the intermittent wars waged between France and Britain. Therefore traders had to have a source of credit they could rely on and a safety net in hard times. Because Scots law recognised business partnerships as separate legal entities, merchants were able to pool resources and protect themselves from some risks. The Tobacco Lords shared commercial information, extended credit to each other and set up their own banks, thereby exerting greater influence as a group than they would have done as competing individuals.

The Oswalds followed the stores and family models and, in 1725, sent their first cousin Richard, later known as Richard of Auchincruive, to be their factor in Virginia, Carolina and Jamaica.[6] He handled all the administration of their business, kept accounts, insurance and business records, and gained valuable experience and contacts. From 1730 to 1740 Richard acted as supercargo for the brothers' merchandise.[7] He

---
5. A minister or elder who is elected to chair the annual General Assembly of the Church of Scotland, and represent the church in Scotland and abroad for the following year.
6. A factor is an agent or bailiff, who was stationed at a port or other trading place.
7. A supercargo (from Spanish sobrecargo) is a person employed on

doubled their profits by ensuring that vessels sailed fully laden in both directions, carrying goods outward that were in demand in the colonies, and tobacco, sugar and wine on their return. It made sense to make a minor detour to import wine from Madeira, a Portuguese island which was a convenient stopping-off point for ships, with its fresh water and access to markets that were not the usual British outlets.

Richard took this trade to its logical extension and became a partner in a Port Glasgow rope factory in 1741 and a bottleworks in 1744: the bottles were on hand when the ships landed their hogsheads of Madeira;[8] and the rope factory, aside from its original purpose of producing the ropes needed on the boats, won concessions to dredge the Clyde and repair the quays. Frugal, hardworking and hard-nosed, the Oswalds carefully chose their goods and markets to create economic synergies and to generate profits from multiple sources. In 1741, the brothers brought their cousin back to Glasgow as a partner, where he combined skilled management of the business with a continued presence in America and the Caribbean.

As competition with France on the high seas was heating up, both the Royal and merchant navies were in great need of men and ships, and one way to attract crews was to offer prize money for captured

---

board a vessel by the owner of cargo carried on the ship. Their duties are defined by admiralty law and include managing the cargo owner's trade, selling the merchandise in ports to which the vessel sails, and buying and receiving goods to be carried on the return voyage. He collected debts, dunned debtors, purchased, packaged and loaded tobacco.

8. Hogsheads were large wooden barrels. A hogshead full of tobacco weighed 1,000 lb. A hogshead of Madeira contained 48 gallons.

vessels. In 1744, on one of his voyages in the West Indies, Richard captured a French ship. The Oswalds sold it and its cargo for a total of £15,000. With the proceeds Richard set up a London operation in 1746, leasing a counting house at 17 Philpot Lane.[9] Close to the Thames, it was a short walk to the warehouses and coffee houses where Richard could bargain, shop around, gather intelligence and network.

The brothers were active members of the Glasgow merchant community and were Burgesses and Guild Brethren of Glasgow. This elevation in rank enabled them to come to the city's aid during the '45 rebellion. In 1715 and 1745, James Stuart and Charles Edward Stuart respectively, the direct descendants of the deposed James II, attempted to seize the throne from the German House of Hanover. They were supported by Scottish clansmen, some English Catholics, Irish and French but not by the majority of the population in England or Scotland. During the first Jacobite rebellion in 1715, the mainly Protestant city of Glasgow sided with the Hanoverians and raised ten companies to fight James' army. The rebellion of 1745 initially met with more success and the Young Pretender, Charles Edward Stuart, marched with 4,000 men south from Glenfinnan on the west coast to

---

9. Eighteenth-century counting houses were a combination of home and office. Richard Oswald's three-storey house had living quarters on the upper floors (housing family and employees) and offices on the ground floor, where Oswald ran his business operations, agreeing contracts for sales, extending credit and sharing commercial information with partners, clients, brokers and ships captains. Philpot Lane now sports a tiny statue of two mice eating cheese, set high on the wall of a nineteenth-century commercial building, to commemorate two workers who fell from there to their deaths.

Leckie, less than forty miles from Glasgow. Glasgow's prosperity tottered. There was widespread panic in the defenceless city, as wild rumours abounded and those who could, fled. The rebels harassed local burghs, businesses closed, payments were halted on bills and tobacco lay in quantities waiting to be shipped.

From his camp at Leckie, Charles wrote to the provost, magistrates and town council of Glasgow that, 'I need not inform you of my being come hither, nor of my view in coming … All those who love their country and the true interest of Britain ought to wish for my success and do what they can to promote it. I hope this is your way of thinking and therefore expect your compliance with my demands.' What the Bonnie Prince demanded was all the arms in the city and £15,000. He continued: 'I choose to make these demands but if not complied with I shall take other measures and you must be answerable for the consequences.'

Since Glasgow's entire annual revenue was £3,000, paying the sum demanded by the Young Pretender would have bankrupted the city. Provost Andrew Cochrane led a delegation of leading councillors, among them Richard and Alexander Oswald, to treat with the Prince's envoy. Although the rout of General Cope's British army on 21 September at Prestonpans had boosted Jacobite confidence, the Prince was willing to negotiate and on 27 September was persuaded to reduce the tribute to £5,500 and £500 worth of goods, including broadswords. As Episcopalians and potential Jacobites, Richard and Alexander were initially suspected of giving financial help to the rebels, but the brothers enhanced their reputation in Glasgow by making a significant contribution to the negotiations and to the ransom, which had to be paid immediately in cash.

The Jacobite Rebellion soon collapsed at Derby, and Charles' retreating army spent a week in Glasgow from 26 December 1745 to 3 January 1746. The Prince, who apparently admired Glasgow, admitted there was no support for him among the populace – indeed, there is said to have been an attempt to shoot him in the Saltmarket. He set up his headquarters in the Trongate and gave grand balls while fining Glasgow and neighbouring Paisley for their lack of support and demanding supplies of clothes and shoes. The council selected Richard Oswald and his fellow citizen John Nelson to provide 12,000 linen shirts.

Charles fled to France and, with the return of stability, Glasgow resumed its commercial and cultural trajectory. Bursting with new ideas and brimming with self-confidence, the Tobacco Lords extended their power over Glasgow itself. These merchants might not have been aristocrats, but for a time they were lords of all they surveyed. They frequented the Glasgow exchanges and coffee shops in their distinctive black tricorn hats, scarlet cloaks and silver-tipped ebony canes, projecting arrogance and power, 'assuming the air and deportment of persons immeasurably superior to all around them'.[10]

By the sett of the burgh of Glasgow of 1711,[11] the council consisted of thirteen merchants and twelve

---

10. Reid and Pagan, *Glasgow Past and Present*.
11. The sett is the constitution or form of government of a Scottish burgh, fixed by charter.

tradesmen, led by the Lord Provost and three baillies (two from the merchant class, the other a trades baillie from the class of mechanics). In the eighteenth century these merchants came overwhelmingly from the ranks of the Tobacco Lords, who dominated the city council and were often able to implement their projects and crush opposition. They did, however, overplay their hands with the Ship Bank.

Until the middle of the eighteenth century there were no banks in Glasgow, so citizens had to travel to Edinburgh to deposit their money, or lodge it with the Tobacco Lords. In 1749, two Tobacco Lords, Dunlop and Houston, set up Glasgow's first regular bank, the Ship Bank,[12] in which the Oswald brothers' second cousin George became a partner in the 1760s. This financial monopoly rankled with other businessmen, who set up a rival Merchant Bank in 1762, in the teeth of opposition from the Tobacco Lords.

Innovators in business, banking, commerce and trade, the Tobacco Lords were instrumental in promoting the new Scottish Bankruptcy Act in 1782. A year later they set up the Chamber of Commerce in Glasgow,[13] which is the oldest in the world after New York's. They formed partnerships and invested in each other's ventures, moving into manufacturing cotton and linen and later shifting their trading focus to the

---

12. So called because of the image of a ship on its banknotes. It was officially Dunlop, Houston & Co, the names of the Tobacco Lords who founded it. The Ship Bank was acquired by the Union Bank of Scotland in 1843.
13. On 31 December 1782, James Oswald wrote to the Lord Provost, 'Mr J. Oswald … sends enclosed some observations on the plan of the Chamber of Commerce, that have occurred to him and his friends'.

East Indies, where they resisted the monopoly of the East India Company.

While focusing on profit, the Tobacco Lords also benefited from and contributed to the Scottish Enlightenment. Unlike in England, where Thomas Cromwell's reformation had stripped the Catholic church of its assets to fill the king's coffers, in Scotland confiscated wealth remained in the community, which invested resources in a humanist-inspired education system. The Scottish Education Act of 1496 had decreed that all sons of barons and freeholders of substance should attend grammar schools. Since the seventeenth century, Lowland Scotland had a network of parish schools teaching standardised lessons, an early type of national curriculum. By 1582 Scotland had four universities compared with two in England, by far the more populous and wealthy country.

Scotland was greatly influenced by ideas from across the North Sea. Through their well-established trade links, Scots followed the discussions on philosophy and economics current in the Netherlands, France and the Baltic states, which helped fuel the Scottish Enlightenment. Although few, if any, of the Tobacco Lords were university educated, they were intellectually curious, and well aware of the commercial and social potential of the new learning. They influenced and supported higher education and sponsored chairs of moral philosophy and humanity at Glasgow University. Several of their number, including Richard's heir George Oswald, were elected Rector of Glasgow University.

This was a period when new worlds were opening up and the demarcation between science, philosophy and economics was less pronounced than in later centuries. Elements of the nascent industrial revolution fed on each other. From the late sixteenth century many people of the 'middling sort' had enough spare purchasing power that fashions in clothes, furniture and accessories were no longer the province of the rich.[14]

By the eighteenth century, the industrial revolution and wage employment meant there was a huge variety of consumer items either manufactured in the new industrial towns or imported from across the oceans. Science and engineering created the factories and processes to manufacture consumer and industrial goods and the transport hardware and infrastructure to move raw materials and finished goods across Europe and the oceans – not only the Atlantic, as the East Indies were opening up. This was to provide opportunities for great wealth from which several Tobacco Lords, and the Oswalds in particular (and eventually Anniesland Hall) would benefit. This openness to new ideas led to new thinking about belief and a widening of theological horizons, which produced the great evangelical movements, to the birth of Anniesland Hall and, eventually, to its demise.

The Tobacco Lords were members and founder members of numerous clubs in Glasgow, such as the Hodge Podge, the Political Economy Club and the Tontine Society (where the Chamber of

---

14. The 'middling sort', originally an Elizabethan term, were people who were not poor but were not gentry.

Commerce met for its first four years).[15] The clubs were originally coffee houses where gentlemen could read newspapers and scientific periodicals and discuss the issues of the day. Papers were read on subjects covering natural science, commerce, improvement – such as the establishment of a police force in Britain 'consistent with Liberty', or 'whether paper credit is beneficial or hurtful to a trading nation'.[16] These were congenial surroundings for the merchant elite to engage in debate, witness demonstrations on natural science or, less formally, network and share trading intelligence over a coffee or a glass of Madeira. Of the ninety colonial merchants who were subscribers to the Tontine Society, twenty (including Richard and Alexander Oswald) were Tobacco Lords. In the Tontine's opulent coffee shop the members, among them several renowned academics – professors of logic, humanity, natural philosophy and moral philosophy – exchanged information and ideas.

The great philosopher and economist Adam Smith was a member of the nearby Political Economy Club, founded in 1743 by Andrew Cochrane, one of the foremost Tobacco Lords. Smith was a regular contributor to debates at the club and in long conversations with Cochrane he gained a deeper insight into the practicalities of mercantilism, free trade and the market economy. He drew on his discussions with Cochrane when writing *The Wealth of Nations*, a treatise on industry and commerce published in

---

15. A tontine is an annuity shared by subscribers to a loan or common fund, the shares increasing as subscribers die until the last survivor enjoys the whole income.
16. Peters, *Glasgow's Tobacco Lords*, pp. 244f.

1776 which is regarded as the first modern work on economics.

Commercial acumen was essential to the optimum exploitation of all the business opportunities that were opening up – and the more those with enquiring minds learnt, the more their ideas could cross-fertilise with others'.

The Tobacco Lords applied the new economic concepts and technology to their business ventures, and their confidence in searching out new ideas led them to diversify their commercial interests and innovate in their home territory. Although they kept their wealth within their families and their group, their money permeated across the community and Scotland as a whole. They became Scotland's richest trading elite and – significantly for the future – they reinvested their wealth in economic growth areas, such as land, shipping, industry and the transformation of Glasgow city centre. They saw that Enlightenment values of reason, progress and order were not reflected in the filthy, narrow, crowded streets of old Glasgow, so they and other merchants moved west of the old High Street and built townhouses in a grid system – now known as the Merchant City – and magnificent neoclassical churches.

One such church, Saint Andrew's-in-the-Square, built between 1739 and 1756, was modelled on St Martin's-in-the Field in London and is considered one of the loveliest neoclassical churches in Britain. The Oswald brothers were prime movers in the establishment of St Andrews-by-the-Green, known as the 'whistlin' kirk' because the organ was played during services.[17] This Episcopalian church did not escape Glasgow sectarianism and the mason Andrew Hunter was excommunicated by the Kirk for 'great sin and scandal on building an Episcopal Meeting House'.

Even more grandly, Tobacco Lord William Cunninghame's Palladian mansion now forms part of the elegant Scottish Gallery of Modern Art in Queen's Street (better known to Glaswegians for the equestrian statue outside, whose rider the Duke of Wellington is never without at least one orange traffic cone on his head). The names of Jamaica Street and Virginia Street in the city centre still bear witness to the sugar and tobacco trades. This was a new, confident, world city built to last. Glasgow's westward expansion continued over the next 200 years, and would benefit the Oswald family and, in the twentieth century, Anniesland Hall.

The Oswald brothers were now prosperous, respected members of an influential group, but they lacked the deep-rooted prestige of the landed aristocracy. In 1751, to establish themselves as landowners, a sure route to respectability and stability, and to provide collateral for loans, the brothers bought the Scotstoun estate to the west of Glasgow, which they extended with their 1759 purchase of the neighbouring Balshagray estate for £4,540. By the time the brothers' great niece Elizabeth added the river front in 1825, the estate, with its orchards, gardens and avenues, was becoming part of the growing city, and ran from the Clyde to what is now Great Western Road, where Anniesland Hall was built in 1908.

---

17. The Church in Scotland was informally known as the Kirk.

Having established the family on a solid footing, Alexander and Richard died without issue, in 1763 and 1766 respectively, and were buried in Glasgow Cathedral. The Scotstoun estate passed to their second cousin George (1735–1819), while their cousin and partner Richard, later known as Richard of Auchincruive (1705–84), continued to diversify and expand the Oswald empire.

2. Richard of Auchincruive:

A tree bearing fruits of good and evil

Despite the physical limitations of poor eyesight and slight deafness, Richard of Auchincruive was restless, ambitious, eager to build on his experience and to turn every challenge into an opportunity. With no legitimate children of his own,[1] he did not fall into the trap of entrusting his business to untried sons, but trained and mentored young men, often from influential families, who went overseas to trade and brought him useful connections in India, China and America. On the basis of commercial intelligence from these associates and from other sources, Oswald was adept at identifying risks and opportunities. He recognised the inherent instability of international trade and mitigated this through diversification and venturing into new markets. An accomplished networker and dealmaker, Oswald advised British businessmen on profitable locations for commercial ventures in the Americas and the East,

---

1. Richard had two sons from a relationship, which may have been a marriage, before meeting Mary Ramsey. He supported both sons until they died in young adulthood.

and introduced them to investment partners who were themselves men of standing in the British and American establishments. He socialised with or was a friend of major power brokers and leading figures of the day, notably, two of the future Founding Fathers, Benjamin Franklin and Henry Laurens, and the writers James Boswell and Laurence Sterne.

While working for his cousins in Jamaica, Richard met and, in 1750, married Mary Ramsay, the sole heir of Alexander Ramsay, who owned property in North America and a sugar plantation in Jamaica. That Mary was alive at the age of thirty-one is evidence of her resilience, as life in Jamaica was cheap and short. One third of whites who came to the Caribbean died within three years, and outcomes were not much better for white people who were born there.[2] Of those who survived childhood, half were dead before they reached forty. This, and the violent and hazardous nature of slave societies, meant that men and women would come to the Caribbean hoping to get rich quick, and return to Europe with their fortunes before they succumbed. It was a world in which many white women survived through prostitution, many male owners and overseers resorted to vicious cruelty and torture to cow the slaves, frequently raping and gang-raping women and girls. The atmosphere was permeated with callousness, drunkenness and a desensitised fatalism. With births and regular imports, slaves far outnumbered whites, who were in constant fear that their brutality would spark a revolt. The author of *Amazing Grace,* John Newton, who

---

2. Parker, *The Sugar Barons*, pp. 292f.

repented of his slave trading and became a convinced abolitionist, saw that 'the real or supposed necessity of treating the Negroes with rigour gradually brings a numbness on the heart'. The staggeringly wealthy plantation owners aped the sophistication of their European counterparts. They built grand houses in landscaped grounds and, arrayed in the latest London or Paris fashions, attended balls and theatres in the elegant quarters of Spanish Town. This was the world which formed Mary, perhaps contributing to her reputed heartlessness, but also giving her the strength and will to follow her husband round the battlefields of Europe.

Marriage to Mary brought Richard Oswald funds, land and connections – another example of his talent for seizing his chances and, like his cousins before him, being in the right place at the right time. And the right time in the mid-eighteenth century was wartime.

The War of Austrian Succession raged across Europe from 1740 to 1748, followed by the Seven Years' War (1756–63), which spanned five continents. These global conflicts involved all the major European powers, presenting business opportunities to the bold. Britain was an ally of Prussia and the armies of both nations needed reliable supplies. Oswald was appointed Chief Commissary of Supplies to the forces in central Europe under the Duke of Brunswick and sent bread and bread wagons to Hessian troops. Armies don't stay in one place. They are constantly on the move, frequently destroying and stealing crops and livestock as they go. When they return, or when they pursue a retreating enemy, they find a ravaged landscape devoid of food or shelter. In winter the fields are bare and in spring farmers do not feel secure enough to plant crops, and so the vicious circle continues. In the Seven Years' War men needed food, but so did horses, who have to graze constantly and will die if deprived of food. Few things were more useless than a dashing cavalryman without a horse – quite unsuited to infantry combat, he was still another mouth to feed. In recent centuries supply logistics have been made easier through telecommunications, which make it possible to locate hungry armies or central food depots, but Richard of Auchincruive had none of this technology. However, he did benefit from his own experience of co-ordinating supply and demand, arranging deliveries of slaves across the seas and, under a government contract, mail, tar and troops to the navy in the Caribbean. He set up and managed bakeries, mills and storehouses west of the Elbe and supplied tobacco, wine, meat and forage to the troops of whichever warring power would pay for it.[3] Richard spent 1758–63 in the war theatre, accompanied for the final three years by Mary. The contacts he gained in this enterprise were invaluable and the profits were stupendous. But the vast sums Richard earnt from his European ventures were dwarfed by his takings from the slave trade.

The plantations of North America and the Caribbean needed legions of labourers, far more than arrived voluntarily, so the first black slaves were brought to Virginia in the 1620s. When European

---

3. Hancock, *Citizens of the World*, pp. 228–30.

2. Richard of Auchincruive: A tree bearing fruits of good and evil

demand for sugar and tobacco rocketed, so did the market in slaves. Oswald had a substantial share in a business partnership, the Company of Merchants Trading to Africa, which operated Bunce Island, off Sierra Leone. With its many islands and small protected bays, abundant in fish, fruits and edible mammals, the Sierra Leone estuary was a haven for merchants and pirates, and the French, Portuguese and Dutch had long traded for slaves there. Until the late 1740s the Royal African Company had a monopoly of the British slave traffic from west Africa and had built a slave entrepôt on Bunce Island. When the government monopoly was lifted, private merchants were encouraged by the African Trade Act of 1750 to step in to meet the rising demand in America for slaves. Oswald and his associates took over Bunce in 1748 and renovated the dilapidated fort, one of the most heavily fortified settlements in west Africa. The entrepôt enjoyed a commercial advantage from managing a fast turnaround for ships, but even this shorter wait was not onerous for senior members of the crew. For the rest and relaxation of the ships' captains waiting for their cargoes,[4] a golf course was created, with African caddies sporting tartan kilts, specially designed and woven in Scotland.

Bunce, a transhipment centre for slaves being sent across the Atlantic and a refuelling point for ships trading in the east, was a vital hub in Richard Oswald's strategy of networking and diversification. The slaves from the island were sent mainly to

---
4. Including John Newton, who docked at Bunce several times in the 1750s.

the Caribbean, where Oswald owned estates in Jamaica, and to Savannah and Charleston. Richard's business partner in Savannah was the rice and indigo planter and slave trader Henry Laurens (1724–92), later one of the Peace Commissioners who went to Paris to negotiate the treaty setting the terms of American Independence. In 1744, Laurens' father had placed him as a trainee in Richard Oswald's London counting house. The two men were friends and business partners for over thirty years, and when Laurens' wife died in the early 1770s, he brought his three children to live in Richard's London home and complete their education. Laurens received a ten per cent commission on every Oswald ship that anchored in Charleston. He earned hefty sums, as rice planters in coastal South Carolina and Georgia were willing to pay high prices for people brought from the 'Rice Coast' of west Africa, who had been growing rice for hundreds of years and were experts at its cultivation and used to tropical conditions.[5]

Oswald watched Laurens' business activities with interest and considered setting up indigo plantations of his own. As an associate of the luminaries of the Scottish Enlightenment, Richard recognised the value of research and scientific enquiry, and carried out agricultural experiments in the glasshouse at his home in Ayrshire. The results were sufficiently promising for him to acquire 20,000 acres of land in Florida

---

5. Because these people were transported from a specific area to a specific area, their descendants, known as the Gullah, can still be identified through genetics and their vocabulary, which contains numerous African words, especially from the languages of Sierra Leone, Guinea and Liberia.

2. Richard of Auchincruive: A tree bearing fruits of good and evil

along the Halifax and Tomoka rivers, fifty miles south of St Augustine. One of the conditions of the land grant was that Oswald should employ European immigrants, but not enough came and he was granted permission to import slaves from Africa. As always, he was willing to give advice to ambitious young men, such as J. Bowman junior who, following an initial letter of introduction from his father, bombarded Oswald with questions:

> Do you think I ought to take out any stock of provisions to serve the workmen or negroes after their arrival in Florida? Can you give me letters of recommendation or credit for Savannah by Charlestown? Can I get good seasoned slaves trained to clearing of ground at either of these places? What kind/quantity of tools should I take out?[6]

Richard advised the young man on how to put in a petition regarding the land he wished to purchase and suggested contacts. One hopes J. Bowman junior, whom his father regarded as a bit of a dilettante, fared better in Florida than did Richard himself. For a time the Mount Oswald plantation produced indigo, rice, timber, molasses, rum, sugar and oranges, but the greenhouse in Ayrshire proved a poor model for the vastly different climate and terrain of subtropical Florida, and Richard never made a profit. In 1785, after Oswald's death, Britain ceded Florida back to Spain and the Mount Oswald plantation was

---
6. Edinburgh University Library Special Collections (EULSC) GB237 Coll 521 5.11.1868.

abandoned. All that remains today is a memorial in the Tomoka State Park.

To modern eyes, it is a mystery that men who embraced Enlightenment values of reason, progress, liberty and fraternity could also countenance slavery. Since biblical times at least, slavery had been an element of many societies. Some Christians deployed selective quotes from the Bible to justify slavery, while others used different (or even the same) texts to demonstrate that the practice was unchristian. There was ample biblical evidence of slavery, cited by some as proof that the practice was endorsed by God, although much that is mentioned in the Bible is abhorred by God. Another circle had to be squared as, when the Israelites were themselves enslaved by the Egyptians they did not regard it as a positive experience. Neither did the thousands of English and Irish people who were captured and enslaved by Barbary Coast traders until well into the eighteenth century.

The morality of slavery had been debated for centuries. Wulfstan, an eleventh-century Archbishop of York, had preached against the export of slaves from Britain, arguing that slavery could only be acceptable if both masters and slaves were Christians, and that slaves would lose their souls if they were sold to heathens. In later centuries, Christian and Muslim slave traders believed that it was unethical to enslave co-religionists, but that pagans were fair game. In the eighteenth and early nineteenth centuries, planters resisted evangelical desires to convert and baptise slaves, claiming that the Protestant requirement of instruction before conversion would lead to rebellion.

2. Richard of Auchincruive: A tree bearing fruits of good and evil

In many plantation societies, slaves were the majority of the population but spoke a wide variety of often mutually incomprehensible African languages. If they received religious instruction in English, they would be able to communicate with other groups and plot rebellion. In *Memoirs of Emma Courtney*[7], a semi-autobiographic novel published in 1796, Mary Hays described a discussion among members of polite society, including a slave owner, on the 'temporary mischiefs which might ensue, in case of an abolition'. These 'mischiefs' were part of a general fear of the upheaval and insecurity that would result from a radical change in the structure of the slave society, or indeed of the colonial society, as Robert Haldane,[8] whose wife inherited Richard's fortune, discovered in 1796 (see Chapter 5).

Slavery was barely visible to the ordinary people of Glasgow at the time – ownership of personal slaves had been banned in England since 1772 and in Scotland since 1778. Although the tobacco merchants' operations were part of the slave triangle, fewer than five slaving ships ever sailed up the Clyde. As late as 1891, Colin Dunlop Donald, grandson of the tobacco merchant Colin Dunlop, asserted that 'there is not a stone in Liverpool that is not cemented with the blood of a slave, but Glasgow, to her honour, kept out of that trade'.[9] He was deluding himself – tobacco and sugar clearly underpinned the city's prosperity and as early as the eighteenth century the slave system on

---

7. Hays, *Memoirs of Emma Courtney*, p. 112.
8. Haldane married Richard's great niece Catherine in 1785.
9. Donald, *Minute Book*, pp. 142–3.

which this wealth relied was increasingly seen to be at odds with the new Britain. The country was becoming wealthier and less brutish; with property to lose, the middling sort began to seek order and stability and had time to consider the world around them. The people of the British Isles were becoming conscious of the notion of society as a whole, rather than restricting their loyalties to the clan, the family and the parish. Since the Reformation (see Chapter 3) many people no longer believed in either the infallibility of the Pope or the divine right of any monarch to pronounce on ethics, so they had to think and discuss among themselves and come to new and sometimes radical conclusions about their place in society, and the place of other peoples and races – and evangelical Christians were in the forefront.

Already in the seventeenth century people had begun to question the morality of slavery and a group of Quakers, led by George Fox, had visited Barbados in 1671. Soon after, Fox published pamphlets appealing for better treatment of slaves – 'Did not Christ taste Death for every man? And are they [the slaves] not Men?'[10] From the 1780s the Abolitionists, led by William Wilberforce, fought in the British parliament to end the slave trade. Theirs were no longer voices crying in the wilderness – in addition to many ordinary people, the anti-slavery movement was attracting prominent adherents from the social and political elite. Methodists, Quakers and celebrities of the day, such as the painter Sir Joshua Reynolds and Samuel Johnson's biographer James Boswell, were

---

10. Parker, p. 153.

2. Richard of Auchincruive: A tree bearing fruits of good and evil

high-profile opponents of slavery. The Lord Chief Justice, Lord Mansfield, stated that 'the status of slavery is so odious that nothing can be suffered to support it but positive law'.

During his lifetime Richard Oswald was clearly aware of the growing unease at this exploitation of human beings. Men close to him were expressing doubts:

- his nephew Alexander Oswald of Shieldhall, who 'would not, directly nor indirectly, mix himself up with slavery'[11] (though how he squared this with being a partner in the South Sugar-House Company is not clear)
- his friends Boswell and Adam Smith (Smith analysed the economics and concluded that 'the work done by slaves … is in the end the dearest of any')
- his fellow British commissioner at the Paris talks, David Hartley. In 1977 Hartley put forward the first resolution against slavery in the House of Commons, stating that 'the slave trade is contrary to the laws of God and the rights of men'
- Washington's aide-de-camp, Henry Laurens' son John (who had spent several years living in Richard's house in London on the death of his mother), is best known for his criticism of slavery and his efforts to recruit slaves to fight against the British in return for their freedom.

---

11. The Hidden Glasgow Forums – hiddenGlasgow.com.

Perhaps Oswald believed his own account that the slaves he purchased were bought, not captured by his agents, and were not abused. Perhaps he was unable to see slaves as humans, although he must have seen acts of nobility and decency from slaves, and heard the sobs of mothers separated from their children. After all, it is unlikely he would have treated his horses as badly as his cargoes of slaves. Perhaps years on the battlefields of Europe, and his wife's upbringing on a slave plantation, had numbed them to suffering. Whatever the explanation, Richard was both a man ahead of his time, and a man outpaced by evolution in society.

When Richard of Auchincruive died in 1784 Bunce Island was inherited by his nephews John and Alexander Anderson. In 1787 British philanthropists led by Granville Sharp, an associate of William Wilberforce, established a settlement twenty miles away where freed or escaped slaves could find refuge. The managers of Bunce Island harassed and abused these campaigners, claiming that they attempted to mitigate the sufferings of their slaves. They pointed out that Oswald had forbidden the use of violence and kidnapping (slaves should be obtained, not by capture, but through barter under his contract with the local African king) and had banned branding, instead putting chequered beads around the slaves' arms. He also insisted that slave families be kept together on the plantations. This was far-sighted and perhaps less altruistic than it might seem – treating slaves humanely made life easier and was less wasteful. Oswald had no control over the treatment of slaves

2. Richard of Auchincruive: A tree bearing fruits of good and evil

once they had been sold, and contributed greatly to the numbers despatched to a miserable death during the voyage or a wretched life on the plantations. Between 1748 and 1784, 12,929 slaves sailed from Bunce Island, two per cent of all exports by traders of all nationalities from the west coast of Africa. Wilberforce and his colleagues eventually prevailed and the Slave Trade Act prohibiting the trade was passed in 1807, with ships' captains subject to a fine per slave found on board. Bunce was now worthless and the Anderson brothers pulled out in 1811.

The Tobacco Lords may have feared slave uprisings, pirates and disease, but a much greater threat to their operations came from within America. The North American colonies were growing apart from Great Britain. Many Americans were educated and articulate, and had originally founded their communities on principle and dissent; they were fiercely protective of their liberties and resentful of British high-handedness. The Tobacco Lords enjoyed huge profits and immense influence over the economy of the colonies, and this was increasing American resentment. Many small planters had no choice but to participate in the Tobacco Lords' stores system (see Chapter 1) because the colonies were forbidden to set up their own industries, making them dependent on British goods. The farmers were not paid for their produce until the vessel transporting the tobacco to Glasgow had made the return trip to Virginia, taking up to several months. As a result, the colonies' trade deficit with Britain grew ever wider, and any cash purchases depleted their gold reserves. There are always individual casualties in a system based on credit, and the tobacco growers in Maryland and Virginia were no exception. Some of the Tobacco Lords took advantage of their financial difficulties and offered them reduced prices for their crop – William Cunninghame was known to offer as much as ten per cent below market value to distressed growers.

The mounting debts incurred by these small farmers was a significant factor in the hostility towards Britain that culminated in the 1776 War of Independence. In 1786 George Washington wrote:

> a powerful engine for [mercantile profiting] was the giving of good prices and credit to the planter till they got him more immersed in debt than he could pay without selling lands or slaves. They then reduced the prices given for his tobacco so that … they never permitted him to clear off his debt.[12]

Far from protecting the planters' fortunes, this behaviour proved short-sighted and counter-productive. As both a landholder in Virginia, Georgia and Florida, and a creditor, Oswald had first-hand knowledge of all the issues at stake. Given the breadth of his experience in America and his considerable standing with its main players, the British government sought Richard's advice throughout the American War of Independence, but he seems to have been powerless to prevent British incompetence, particularly that of the Governor of Virginia, Lord Dunmore, from pushing the colonists over the edge.

12. Breen, *Tobacco Culture*, pp. 119–22.

2. Richard of Auchincruive: A tree bearing fruits of good and evil

By 6 March 1776 Richard was receiving alarming intelligence from his nephew and agent Alexander Oswald that Norfolk and Gosport in Virginia had been destroyed.

> The provincials' had fired on British ships, so the king's men had set that part of the town on fire, and the provincials burned the rest. Friends of the government went on the ships. Not many slaves joined Lord Dunmore.[13] It is the general opinion here that many of the people in Virginia will show themselves friends to Government when they can be protected – but I am afraid the protection that our army can afford will not be so safe as to induce these people to take a side.[14]

In February 1777 Alexander, who was monitoring the movement of Oswald's ships from New York, reported that 'the people in general are still as violent as ever – particularly in the southern colonies'. On 13 March 1777 Alexander sent 'news of rebel attacks on our troops. They are very troublesome to our people when they find them in small numbers'.[15]

When the British were defeated at Yorktown in 1781 it was clear that America would win its independence, but there was debate on how this should be achieved. The charismatic orator and anti-

---
13. In 1755 Dunmore had promised freedom to any slaves who fled their masters and fought loyally for Great Britain. This had enraged more colonials than it had attracted runaway slaves.
14. EULSC, Coll 521, 6.3.1776.
15. EULSC, Coll 521, 13.3.1777.

slavery campaigner Charles James Fox was appointed Foreign Secretary in 1782. Fox, who supported the American patriots, had advocated unconditional independence for the colonies. The new Prime Minister Lord Shelburne, who sympathised with the American patriots and had been against the war in the first place, wanted it to be contingent on a treaty with the Americans' Spanish and French allies, who were hoping to gain territory in Gibraltar and Canada. Founding Fathers John Jay and Benjamin Franklin had set as a precondition for the talks that Britain explicitly acknowledge the nationhood of the American colonies. Shelburne realised that British dominion over these colonies was a lost cause and was alert to the dangers of antagonising the Americans and pushing them further into the arms of the French. For him, the ultimate prize was a profitable two-way trading relationship.

To this end, Britain planned to be magnanimous, but France, which had fought with the Americans against the British, and Spain saw an opportunity to capitalise on Britain's defeat. American and French privateers attacked the Clyde during the war of independence, and on 19 July 1779 William Burne wrote from the east coast of Scotland to Richard Oswald:

> for some days this coast has been much alarmed with the appearance of several ships of force by some supposed to be Paul Jones Squadron, while other accounts say he is upon the west coast. Be that as it will a 50-gun ship and frigate and a cutter

2. Richard of Auchincruive: A tree bearing fruits of good and evil

sailed along Kirkcaldy Bay near Inchkeith. They tacked about turning, drove back by a strong westerly wind. We now learn they have [left] for the French coast. We had no force to oppose them.[16]

Spain, later supported by the French navy, blockaded Gibraltar from June 1779 to February 1783. In these circumstances the British government could not be seen to be suing for peace with the Americans, but Shelburne arranged for an American delegation to come to Paris for private negotiations. He instructed Richard Oswald to act as chief negotiator. In his letter of introduction to Franklin, Shelburne wrote:

> I have had a longer acquaintance with him than even I have had the pleasure to have with you. I believe him an honest man, and after consulting some of our common friends, I have thought him the fittest for the purpose. He is a practical man and conversant in those negotiations which are most interesting to mankind. This has made me prefer him to any of our speculative friends, or to any person of higher rank.[17]

In a June 1782 entry in his *Journal of Negotiations for Peace*, Franklin wrote 'Mr Oswald seems quite plain and sincere … a wise and honest man'.

Mindful of public opinion, Oswald had to stand firm in the face of Franklin's legendary charm and

---
16. EULSC, Coll 521, 19.7.1779.
17. Hancock, Citizens of the World p. 391.

the Americans' insistence that acknowledgement of their independence was a prerequisite for the talks. In the end, Oswald's steadfastness paid off. Increasingly suspicious of their French and Spanish allies, Jay and Franklin decided to negotiate directly with Britain and dropped their preconditions. Richard Oswald obtained his government's agreement to reword the terms for the negotiations so as to recognise the American commissioners as plenipotentiaries of the United States. After numerous engagements in which Robert Haldane, who later married Oswald's great niece and eventual heir, fought with distinction, the British navy finally broke the siege of Gibraltar. The British delegates became more confident and assertive, but also more accommodating. Various stumbling blocks were removed and John Jay, Benjamin Franklin, John Adams, Henry Laurens and Richard Oswald signed the Preliminary Articles of Peace on 30 November 1782. These were ratified, almost unchanged, in the Treaty of Paris on 3 September 1783.

The terms were generous to the Americans, prompting some in Britain to complain that Oswald had given too much away. Many people felt that Oswald was too close to the American delegates. Oswald had indeed admitted to Franklin, as recently as May 1782, that the United Kingdom was weak and financially unstable, telling him that 'our enemies may do what they please with us. They have the ball at their foot'.[18] In addition, Oswald had previously exchanged letters with Franklin, who had similar views to his on free trade. Franklin, who gave Oswald

---
18. Morris, *The Peacemakers*, p. 276.

his portrait, described Richard as a man with an 'air of great simplicity and honesty'.

Oswald further compromised himself with the opposition when his friend of thirty years, Henry Laurens, at the time the American minister to the Netherlands, which was part of the Armed Neutrality alliance, was captured by the British navy at sea and imprisoned in the Tower of London in 1780. Laurens was the only American to be sent to the Tower. Together with the statesman and philosopher Edmund Burke, Oswald put up £50,000 to obtain Laurens' release, in exchange for General Lord Cornwallis, whereupon Laurens returned to Amsterdam to raise funds for the American war effort. But Shelburne had appointed Oswald precisely because of his knowledge of American geography and his good relations with the Americans, and in the view of their sovereign, George III, Richard Oswald of Auchincruive was the 'fittest instrument for the renewal of … friendly intercourse' with the colonies.[19]

When Shelburne fell from power in 1783 Oswald lost his place on the commission, his patron and any chance of a peerage. Exhausted, he retired from public life and died at Auchincruive on 6 November 1784.

History's judgment of Oswald's peace terms is less harsh than that of his contemporaries. Shelburne was prescient in advocating minor concessions to obtain the greater, long-term prize of a lucrative transatlantic trade relationship. Despite the War of 1812, the two nations have been close allies in several conflicts and, in 2018, the United States

---
19. Quoted in Hancock, p. 391.

was Britain's largest single-country export market (excluding the EU as a whole).

Yet history will judge Oswald harshly for his huge contribution to slavery. While many merchants grew rich from trading in tobacco, sugar and opium, which have caused significant illness and death over the long term, these commodities did not attract opprobrium at the time. The morality of slavery, on the other hand, had been widely disputed since at least the seventeenth century. Glasgow is coming to terms with the origins of much of its wealth, and will not spare Richard Oswald.

One man who had no time for Richard of Auchincruive was Robert Burns. When Oswald's widow Mary died in 1788, Burns, who was sheltering from a snowstorm in Baillie Whigham's Inn in Sanquhar, was forced to leave when her funeral cortege arrived, and had to ride a further ten miles in the snow. Never one to stint on vitriol, Burns penned an Ode addressed to Richard the 'plunderer of armies', imagining the Tobacco Lord witnessing the arrival in the underworld of Mary, 'that venerable votary of iron avarice and sordid pride':

> Dweller in yon dungeon dark,
> Hangman of creation, mark!
> Who in widow-weeds appears
> Laden with unhonoured years,
> Noosing with care a bursting purse,
>
> Baited with many a deadly curse?
> View the wither'd beldam's face:
> Can thy keen inspection trace

2. Richard of Auchincruive: A tree bearing fruits of good and evil

Aught of humanity's sweet, melting grace?
Note that eye, 'tis rheum o'erflows –
Pity's flood there never rose.
See those hands, ne'er stretched to save,
Hands that took but never gave.
Keeper of Mammon's iron chest,
Lo, there she goes, unpitied and unblest,
She goes, but not to realms of everlasting
   rest!

Plunderer of Armies! Lift thine eyes
(A while forbear, ye torturing fiends),
Seest thou whose step, unwilling, hither
   bends?
No fallen angel, hurled from upper skies!
'Tis thy trusty, quondam Mate,
Doomed to share thy fiery fate:
She, tardy, hell-ward plies.
And are they of no more avail,
Ten thousand glittering pounds a year?
In other worlds can Mammon fail,
Omnipotent as he is here?

O bitter mockery of the pompous bier!
While down the wretched vital part is driven
The cave-lodged beggar, with a conscience
   clear,
Expires in rags, unknown, and goes to
   Heaven.

There are reports that Mary was indeed, as Burns wrote, 'detested with the most heartfelt cordiality' by her tenants and servants and had a reputation for being tight-fisted. But Burns' poem should not be taken purely as a principled attack on people who had earned their fortunes through slavery (which in any case is not specifically mentioned in the ode). In 1786 the impoverished Burns had himself been preparing to emigrate and work as a bookkeeper on a friend's sugar plantation in Jamaica, which depended on the forced labour and harsh treatment of black slaves. Fate intervened at the last minute, as Burns' *Poems* were published to great acclaim and his financial situation secured. The 'Ode to Mary Oswald' was inspired partly by her reputation and partly by the poet's pique at being forced out into the snowy night. Later, when he was lionised by society, Burns admitted that he felt considerably less hostile to 'these great folks whom I have now the honour to call my acquaintances, the Oswald family'.[20]

Now fabulously wealthy, Richard was able to take a step towards membership of the landed gentry. In the mid-1700s various commercial banks failed, including at least one in Ayr. As a result, owners of estates in Ayrshire who had shares and deposits in these banks had to sell up, presenting Richard with the opportunity to purchase the Auchincruive estate in Ayrshire in 1764. The surviving Adams-designed rooms at Auchincruive House are spacious, elegant and delicately ornamented. Richard's letters to tenants and supplicants show a man respectful and generous to people in need, hard to square with the ruthlessness a man would need to prosper in the brutal worlds in which he had made his fortune.[21]

---

20. Martin, *Auchincruive*, p. 182.
21. EULSC, Coll 521.

2. Richard of Auchincruive: A tree bearing fruits of good and evil

As proprietor of Auchincruive, Richard had the patronage of nearby St Quivox church, which dates back to the thirteenth century. In 1767 he funded and oversaw extensive refurbishment to the building, adding a burial vault, where he and Mary lie. Oswald's renovations included an elegant, curved auditorium for the congregation, with polished pine pews formerly allocated to separate trades, a gallery for a local landed family and, facing the pulpit, the Auchincruive gallery. This is fitted with front rows of capacious seating for the family, upholstered with red velvet, while the hard wooden pews behind are for the servants, who whiled away the time scratching images in the backs of the family's pews, some of them depicting top-hatted gents. Richard also seems to have needed an escape from the sermonising – to the left of the gallery and invisible from the pulpit is a fireplace, with an armchair where he could retreat and warm himself when he had had enough. He clearly did not share the religious fervour of the time – that would come with later generations of Oswalds and spur them to build and fund Anniesland Hall.

Richard of Auchincruive was not an ostentatious man and used his vast wealth to support small local projects, which have not added lustre to his name in history but which ushered in improvements, many of commercial benefit not only to himself but also for fellow Scots in his own and future generations, and none more so than the Forth and Clyde canal. Although Glasgow is only about forty miles from the Firth of Forth, ships going from coast to coast had to take the long and hazardous route round the north of Scotland. From the early 1760s the Forth and Clyde Canal Company had lobbied to have a canal built to join the two rivers. This was approved by Act of Parliament in 1768 and construction began in earnest, but due to lack of funds the work stopped just north of Glasgow in 1775. In 1777 Richard stepped in with fellow Glasgow merchants and contributed considerable sums which, together with the proceeds from the forfeiture of Jacobite estates, facilitated completion of the canal in 1790, providing a clear route from the Atlantic and the Americas to the North Sea and northern Europe. For a maritime trader like Richard of Auchincruive this made perfect commercial sense; for his heirs, with lands rich in clay, coal and ironstone running from the river Clyde, through Anniesland to the Forth and Clyde canal, it was the final piece in the jigsaw.[22] Anniesland Hall would be a beneficiary 200 years after Richard's death, when the wealth accumulated by a man of vision, with an openness to ideas and influences, and a willingness to participate in major world events, would fund a church which turned increasingly inwards and rejected the wider world.

---

22. Ironstone contains a substantial proportion of an iron ore compound from which iron can be smelted commercially.

2. Richard of Auchincruive: A tree bearing fruits of good and evil

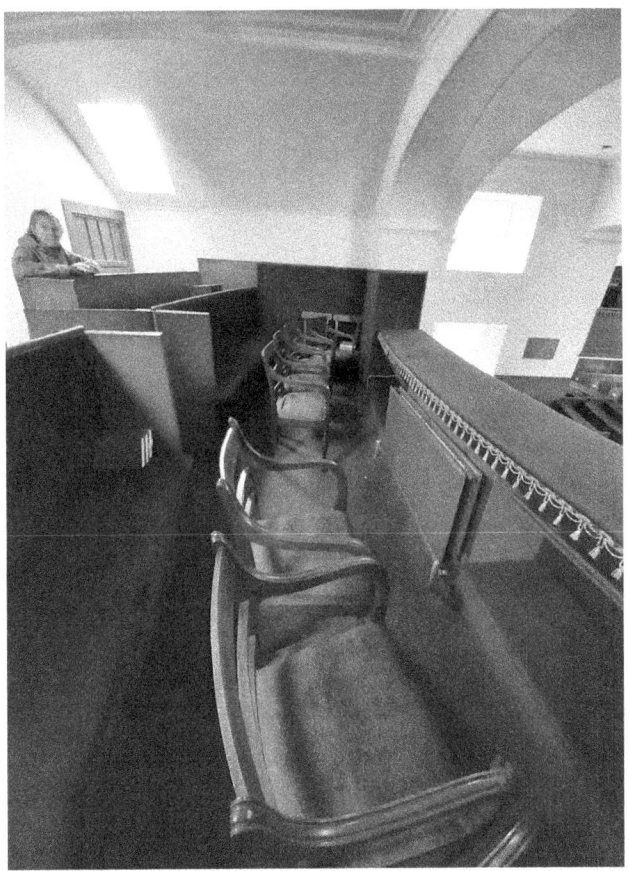

1. The gallery in Auchincruive church with, at the end, Richard's armchair

3. George Oswald of Scotstoun and His Heirs

On Richard's death, Auchincruive was left to his nephew George who, having already inherited the Scotstoun estate, proved to be the happy beneficiary of both family wealth and family failure to produce heirs.

George's career was less swashbuckling than his uncle's. He carried on the family business without major changes. He part-owned a sugar plantation on Grenada and the 'moiety of the negroes' attached to it, he was a partner in the Ship Bank and became head of Oswald, Dennistoun and Co in 1771, which in that year imported tobacco to the value of £1,701,000 (about £340 million in today's money). George enjoyed the life of a wealthy merchant, living comfortably, if relatively uneventfully, and regularly purchased for his personal use silverware, wine, tea, cheese and liqueur – staples of the eighteenth-century well-to-do.[23]

George Oswald was a member of the Board and Green Cloth, one of the more convivial clubs,

23. Peters, pp. 360–62.

which met on Tuesdays from May to November. The membership consisted mainly of merchants, landowners, financiers and their wives, and was less rigorously intellectual than some. It was billed as a whist and supper club, where copious amounts of rum or whisky were consumed before and after a light supper of relatively modest dishes such as Welsh rabbit [sic], Finnan haddies or tripe. Before the evangelicals stepped in, gambling was all the rage and wagers were an additional entertainment at the Board and Green Cloth. After losing a bet, George Oswald stood a dinner and supper costing £20 12s 11½d for Robert Bogle, eldest son of the Tobacco Lord George Bogle. All wagers were duly noted in the Club minutes, as some would take months to be decided:

> May 1809: Mr. Blackburn says that Bathz and St. Martins in or immediately above South Beveland are the same,[24] Mr. Dunlop says, no. — A bottle of rum.
> 16 January 1810: Mr. Blackburn betts a bottle of Rum and five Guineas dry that Mrs N. Brown is not with child at this time. W. Corbet says, yes. Col. C. lost. Settled.
> 20 February 1810: Mr. Carnegie betts a bottle of Rum and a Guinea dry with Mr. Middleton that the French are in possession of Cadiz on or before the first of April next. Mr. C. Lost. Money Paid.[25]

In the early 1770s George's status as a society figure was confirmed when he and his wife had their

---
24. On the Dutch island of Tholen.
25. Donald, pp. 10, 13, 15.

portraits painted by Gainsborough and was further burnished when he was elected Rector of Glasgow University in 1797. When the Bogle family fell on hard times George Oswald and Archibald Smith of Jordanhill bought their Whiteinch estate, adjoining the Scotstoun land, for £15,000 (about £2 million today). It was mainly moorland, but the Oswald family would benefit from what lay beneath – ironstone, coal and an abundance of clay.

When George Oswald died at Scotstoun in 1819 he could have hoped that with five of his thirteen children surviving, the succession was secured.

Richard Alexander Oswald

The estates went to his eldest son, Richard Alexander Oswald of Auchincruive, who proved to be a respected, innovative and generous steward. Although Robert Burns appeared less impressed when he wrote the politically motivated Heron Ballads of 1795:

> An' there'll be wealthy young Richard.
> Dame Fortune should hing by the neck:
> For prodigal thriftless bestowing
> His merit had won him respect.

In 1793 Richard married the celebrated beauty Louisa, or Lucy, Johnston, whom Burns hailed as 'that incomparable woman' – now that he had been accepted into polite society he was happy to heap praise on some of its members. In May 1795 the poet dedicated a song to Lucy. Considerably blander than the 1788 hatchet job on Mary Oswald, these lyrics fell into the one-size-fits-all category:[26]

> Now haply down yon gay green shaw
> She wanders by yon spreading tree.
> How blest ye flowers that round her blaw!
> Ye catch the glances o' her e'e.
> For, while life's dearest blood is warm,
> Ae thought frae her shall ne'er depart,
> And she, as fairest is her form,
> She has the truest, kindest heart.

Lucy had a delicate loveliness, as seen in her portrait by Sir Henry Raeburn, currently in the National Gallery of Scotland. Alas, the fate of many a celebrated beauty caught up with her, and she died of consumption in Lisbon in 1797, leaving two children, Margaret and Richard. Richard had the body of his beloved wife embalmed and brought back to be buried in the family crypt at St Quivox.

In 1817 Richard married Lady Lilias Montgomerie, daughter of the 12th Earl of Eglinton, the Whig MP for Ayrshire between 1780 and 1796. When Eglinton became Lord Lieutenant for Ayrshire in 1796 his brother James succeeded him as MP for Ayrshire from 1818 to 1829. This connection by marriage was commercially and politically advantageous to Richard Oswald, who was now well-placed to enter politics.

---

26. 'None who ever had the delight of seeing her in the ballroom, giving double charms to a minuet, or dignifying a country-dance, can question the truth of this feeble encomium.' Charles K. Sharpe, quoted in *Traditional Tune Archive*.

Richard's parliamentary career had a shaky start. Burns had been perceptive in highlighting his 'prodigal thriftless bestowing' – in 1826, despite his inherited wealth and his connections, Richard became financially 'embarrassed' and moved temporarily to a property he owned in Esher, Surrey. His solvency and his eligibility for parliament were rescued partly by the compensation awarded to Lilias' family when the British government abolished slave ownership in its colonies in 1833. Compensation amounting to £20 million – forty per cent of the Treasury's annual spending budget, and worth nearly £3 trillion in 2022 – was paid to 3,000 families, including the Montgomeries, for loss of their 'property', that is, slaves. Richard and Lilias, her sister and her brother-in-law shared £4,580 for the 255 slaves on the Pemberton Valley estate in Jamaica. Richard was able to return to Ayrshire, where he was Whig MP from 1832 to 1835, which meant that for a time there were two Whig Oswalds in parliament.

Richard had been close to his brother, Royal Navy Captain James Oswald, who served in the Napoleonic war, and they corresponded frequently,[27] but although James survived the war, he died without issue in 1822. Richard's son also predeceased him in 1833. Richard died in the elegant Swiss resort

---

27. In a letter to Richard dated 5 February 1808, James updated his brother on his progress during the Napoleonic war: 'the confirmation of the Rockford Squadron having passed up the Mediterranean is just received and I am to sail this night with all the troops (now in transport here) for Sicily. Which we fear is much in want of troops, and whence the French fleet must ultimately be destined for' – *EULSC 5.2.1808*

of Vevey in 1841 and left the Scotstoun estate to his sister Elizabeth, while his cousin James Oswald (1779–1853) inherited Auchincruive.

James Oswald

James and his brother, Richard Alexander Oswald of Moore Park, carried on the family tradition of international trade by forming the cotton merchants Oswald, Stevenson & Co. After brother Richard died in 1821 James lost a significant amount of money speculating in cotton, with one of his companies filing for bankruptcy and leaving numerous creditors.

These financial difficulties briefly interrupted James' parliamentary career. In 1832 he had been elected as Whig Member of Parliament for Glasgow but was obliged to resign his seat in 1837. This was a temporary setback and when his creditors had been paid in full James was re-elected to parliament, where he served until his retirement in 1847. One of his main motives for entering politics was to further the cause of constitutional reform – since at least 1829 he had been one of the leading campaigners for the 1832 Reform Act. Not all his family shared his enthusiasm. His female relations followed parliamentary proceedings with interest and in a letter to James' sister, his grandmother commented that 'as to whether the Reform Bill will do good to the country I think it doubtful – it certainly will not do the good that is expected'.[28] Over the longer term, the extended

28. EULSC, 7.12.1831.

family (and, later, Anniesland Hall) would benefit from one of James Oswald's achievements. In 1836 he steered the New Anniesland Turnpike Act through parliament, which meant that public transport would run as far as Anniesland, increasing the value of any properties built there.

James Oswald was a conscientious member of parliament and served on several select committees.[29] He lived mainly at Aix-les-Bains in Savoie, France, and in Ardrossan, a small town twenty miles from the Auchincruive estate, which he never occupied. He was described as a 'steady, consistent, honourable man', 'his straightforward manly character commanded universal confidence, while his lively sense of the ludicrous, remarkable memory, quaint anecdote and knowledge of the British classics rendered him a delightful companion'.[30]

James did not marry, but seems to have had at least one delightful companion. During his time out of office, perhaps seeking solace after his financial problems and ejection from politics, he had a close relationship with a French woman, Victorine, in Paris. On 2 November 1838 Victorine wrote him an intimate letter in French, full of tender concern for the well-being and peace of mind of 'mon ange'.[31]

Foreign amours notwithstanding, when Oswald died in 1847 his body was returned to Glasgow where

---

29. Select Committees check and report on areas ranging from the work of government departments to economic affairs. The results of these inquiries are public, and many require a response from the government.
30. Butterfield, *Diary and Autobiography of John Adams*
31. EULSC, 2.11.1838.

he was buried in the cathedral with full honours. Oswald Street, near the Clyde in Glasgow, is named after him, and a statue to him was erected in George Square, where he keeps company with Robert Burns, Robert Peel, William Gladstone and Queen Victoria.

His nephew Alexander Haldane Oswald inherited the Auchincruive estate.

Alexander Haldane Oswald

Alexander's parents both died before his twelfth birthday, but he was surrounded by a loving, supportive family.

The Oswalds, and their in-laws the Haldanes/ Gordon Oswalds, had an extensive and intimate family network, nurtured by shared business interests and the influence of their women, who visited one another, corresponded with each other, shared political insights and guided their menfolk.

When Alexander travelled for his health to Madeira and the south of France, he was showered with solicitous, loving letters from his grandmother and aunts. The letters contained family news – 'we have had a call of Mrs Gordon from Scotstoun'.[32] 'Mrs Wilson, Isabella, [James' cousin] and Mrs [Haldane] Gordon came up from Auchingray [Robert Haldane's estate] … Mrs Anderson and Miss Oswald are expected at Scotstoun… Lady Mary Oswald went up to London'. But there were admonitions too.

---

32. Margaret, daughter of Robert Haldane (see Chapter 5); EULSC 28.10.1829.

James' grandmother, while interested in the manners of the people he met and the characteristics of the countries he visited, took the opportunity to express a hope that his Portuguese and French were improving and that he was 'not trifling away your time'. When Alexander went to Oxford his grandmother's letters echoed missives from grannies across the ages: 'I need not caution you against rashly forming friendships ... earthly pleasures ... camel through the eye of a needle ...'

Alexander responded politely to all correspondence, and sent a detailed account of Queen Victoria's coronation to his aunt, Miss Elizabeth Oswald,[33] at Saltcoats – 'I am just going to dine with Lord Canning – I have seen my uncle William'.[34]

While deeply religious, these ladies were also passionately interested in novels and politics. In December 1831 Alexander's sister, Margaret Dundas Oswald, received a letter from another sister, Mary, discussing James Fenimore Cooper's latest novel before returning to the issues of the day:

> I do think you will find it rather difficult to reconcile your tory principles with affection to young Napoleon. ... If the house of Orleans are driven from the throne (as they ought to be) they [the supporters of the young Henri d'Artois, duc de Bordeaux][35] certainly can make no attempts to regain it

---

33. Heir to the Oswald fortune, (see Chapter 3)
34. EULSC, 29.6.1838.
35. Henri (1820–83) was disputed king of France for one week in 1830, and thereafter pretender to the French throne.

for the French. People have at least as good a right to banish them as Charles X[36]

One of the joys of historical research is to find that 'twas ever thus'. In 1835 Alexander's grandmother wrote to him in Rome that conservatives and reformers were nasty to each other and did injustice to both sides. 'I believe the conservatists [sic] are as honest and sincere as the reformers. Your uncle and Mr Oswald of Auchincruive think likewise'.[37] Such observations did not deter Alexander, who served as Conservative MP for Ayrshire over 1843–52.

These were people who took an intelligent and active interest in public affairs. They were wealthy and educated, products of the Scottish Enlightenment and the Victorian elite, who regarded themselves as residents of North Britain rather than Scotland, comfortable in Britain and on the continent. They had their portraits painted by renowned artists, enjoyed contemporary writers and thinkers and embraced the culture and innovations of the day. To them, the world was a source of fascination, experiences and ideas, which they implemented in their estates and in politics, believing it was their duty to serve the country and to promote democracy and nineteenth-century liberal principles. These Oswalds were pillars of the established church, devout but not dogmatic.

---

36. EULSC, 7.12.1831.
37. EULSC, 6.7.1835.

The Haldanes

After an evangelical interval with Robert Haldane and James Alexander Haldane (see Chapter 5) the Haldanes continued the liberal tradition over the generations. Among them were Naomi Mitchison, writer and feminist, and her paternal uncle, the 'philosopher-politician' Richard, First Viscount Haldane.[38] After a stellar career in Liberal cabinets Viscount Haldane joined the first Labour Government under Ramsay McDonald on the grounds that he was 'moved by the ideal of more complete and general equality of opportunity with which that party was associated'.[39] As a young man Haldane had publicly announced that he would have no connection with any church, and he maintained that position.[40] This contrasted sharply with the Scotstoun Haldane Oswalds, who embraced the evangelical movement and the Free Church of Scotland, and whose convictions underpinned the development of Anniesland Hall.

---

38. Haldane supported Oscar Wilde in his travails and used his influence to have the poet and dramatist moved from Wandsworth to Reading Jail, where he encouraged Wilde to continue writing.
39. R.B. Haldane, *Richard Burdon Haldane*, p. 312.
40. Haldane did have at least one close encounter with the Plymouth Brethren. He was a Junior at the trial of the Launceston Close Brethren community. A young man who had inherited a large fortune in 1886 was persuaded by his tutor, a member of the Close Brethren, to transfer £140,000 (around £24 million in 2022) to the Launceston community. The young man, who had long had mental health issues, committed suicide shortly after. His family brought an action to recover the money on the grounds that the tutor had exercised undue influence while in a position of trust; R.B. Haldane, p. 23.

4. The Reformation and the Evangelicals

Nations are formed by their geography and their external relations, and Scotland was no exception. For some purposes, Scotland can be divided into two sections: the then Gaelic-speaking Highlands and Western Isles; and the Lowlands and the East Coast. The beautiful highlands and islands are the Scotland loved by tourists; the Lowlands and the east coast are home to four respected and ancient universities – St Andrews, Glasgow, Aberdeen and Edinburgh – and to heavy industry and trade. Overseas trade was a significant element in eastern Scotland's economic and cultural development, as the country has the sea on three sides. On the fourth side is the land border with England, already in the fifteenth century the most united, self-consciously developed kingdom in Europe.[1] England's poorer, smaller northern neighbour tended to define itself as 'not English'. The effects of this were both negative – a chronic chip on Scottish shoulders – and positive, as Scotland was particularly receptive to ideas brought over by its northern European trading partners. In the

---
1. MacCulloch, *Reformation*, p. 100.

sixteenth century these ideas mainly concerned new religious thinking.

In central and northern Europe, the dominance of the Roman Catholic Church over ideas, learning and material wealth was weakening. Until the fifteenth century only priests had access to bibles laboriously transcribed in Latin by monks. The Church directly and indirectly controlled secular and religious life and thought, up until 1439 when Gutenberg revolutionised printing presses by developing a combination of suitable inks, a reusable mould and an alloy which kept its shape under pressure. As a result, multiple copies of the scriptures and religious writings could be printed, often in the vernacular. For the first time lay people could read the bible in their own language. The humanist scholar, Desiderius Erasmus, produced a translation of the New Testament that raised doubts about some church doctrines, as he demonstrated they had been based on previous mistranslations from the Greek. In particular, his translation did not include the perpetual virginity of the Virgin Mary, nor the idea that Mary – and by extension the saints – could intercede with God on behalf of the faithful. This provoked criticism of Erasmus, as accepted 'truths' like purgatory or the efficacy of worshipping relics or asking saints to intercede in heaven were considerable money-spinners for the Church. Erasmus was a questioner, not a revolutionary, and was tolerant of other views, but as the Church fought back and executed heretics, the debate became polarised. Martin Luther became more absolute, declaring that the Pope was the Antichrist. Churches in the Baltic

4. The Reformation and the Evangelicals

states tended towards Lutheranism, with which Scottish merchants and universities became familiar through the well-established trade links.

Even so, it was not a Lutheran but a Calvinist, John Knox, who led the Reformation in Scotland. Although Calvinists and Lutherans were fierce antagonists, they did agree on the depravity of mankind and the certainty of eternal damnation for all but the Elect, who were predestined to be chosen by God and were saved through grace alone – not through works, indulgences or the intervention of a priest. Fired up by Knox, in whose opinion rule by a woman was 'monstrous' – that is, unnatural – the Scots rose up against the intelligent and gifted, but feckless, Mary, Queen of Scots, and established the Church of Scotland, or the Kirk. Unlike its Anglican counterpart the Kirk abolished bishops and formal elements of the church hierarchy – the Moderator of the Church of Scotland is elected every year, rather than being appointed by the monarch, and the Kirk derives its authority from its covenant with God.

In August 1560 the Scottish parliament met in Edinburgh, approved a Reformed Confession of Faith (the Scots Confession) and passed several acts pertaining to religion. These reduced the sacraments to two, baptism and communion, and ended the jurisdiction of the Pope in Scotland. Celebration of Mass was now liable to punishment, in some cases by death.[2] Christmas was abolished in 1561. This was Protestantism red in tooth and claw.

---

2. Mackie, Lenman and Parker, *A History of Scotland*, p. 153.

Dispensing with the intercession of priests or saints opened a more direct line from individuals to their God, leaving them less reliant on the Church to interpret God's will or man's place in the universe. The truth was to be found not in the words of a priest nor in papal edicts, but in the Bible, the Word of God. Statues and paintings, which had provided inspiration for the faithful, were banned, as the Word took centre stage. Congregations were now expected to understand and absorb complex and abstract material as church ministers expounded at length on the implications of the most obscure chapters of Holy Writ. This produced a literate and intellectually confident generation who also, while accepting they were sinners justified only by God's grace, felt entitled to decide for themselves on many issues, once the preserve of the papacy.

In Scotland this Calvinist self-confidence, verging on arrogance, produced an intolerance that would result in multiple sects and schisms, the Bishops' Wars, the Covenanters, and the Solemn League and Covenant whose adherents supported parliament in the first English Civil War. It would also prepare the ground for the Plymouth Brethren to interpret the scriptures at will.

On the other hand, this self-confidence empowered Scots to question received wisdom and embrace new ideas in science, philosophy and economics that were arriving from across the North Sea. In the eighteenth century this flowered in the Scottish Enlightenment, which opened up new horizons, both intellectual and geographical, and

4. The Reformation and the Evangelicals

encouraged, as we have seen, debate and innovation in Scottish society in general, including among the Tobacco Lords.

By the eighteenth century, now that the Tobacco Lords had made their fortunes, they could focus on the intellectual preoccupations of the day. The nineteenth century was an age of scientific enquiry and experimentation in which Enlightenment questioning of accepted wisdom opened up vast possibilities for the material improvement of the human condition. This spirit of reappraisal included looking anew at the universe and the concept of an interventionist creator. Some evangelical scholars, such as William Cunninghame the younger, resisted this particular trend and used the new knowledge to prove the absolute literal truth of the Bible.

Before he died in 1799, William Cunninghame the elder, he whose profiteering had been a factor in the rebellion of the American colonies (see Chapter 2), disinherited his two older sons from his first marriage and left his vast fortune and estate to his third son, William. After some years in the Bengal Civil Service, William the younger returned to Scotland and devoted his life to improvements on his estate, biblical study and the premillennialist movement, which also attracted John Nelson Darby, one of the founding members of the Plymouth Brethren (see Chapter 5).[3] In the tradition of Bishop Usher – who, in 1654, drew on his extensive knowledge of ancient history

---

3. On the basis of their literal interpretation of Revelation 20:1–6, premillennialists believe that Jesus will physically return to Earth before the Millennium and reign for a 1,000-year golden age of peace.

and languages, the Bible, astronomy and chronology to identify the time of the Creation as 6.00 p.m. on 22 October 4004 BC – Cunninghame asserted that the reign of the Antichrist had begun in 533 AD. Like many evangelicals, then and later, he pored over the scriptures and marshalled current archaeological and geological discoveries to demonstrate that accounts in the Bible were factual. On that assumption, it followed that biblical prophesies were also credible and that political and natural events have been foretold and fulfil a prophesy or are a direct result of divine or satanic intervention, or both. His many published works included such uncompromising titles as *The Apostasy of the Church of Rome, and the Identity of the Papal Power with the Man of Sin and son of perdition of St. Paul's prophecy.*

With due respect to his scholarship, William's main contribution to this story is his victory in the Stewarton case in 1839. Under the Church Patronage (Scotland) Act of 1711 the principal landowner in each parish – in Cunninghame's case, Stewarton in Ayrshire – had the right to propose suitably qualified candidates for the position of parish minister in the event of a vacancy. The Church of Scotland resented this encroachment on its authority and in 1826 the Kirk Session refused to allow William Cunninghame to take holy communion because, unordained and therefore unqualified, he had been teaching at the Sunday School he had established in the Cunninghame Institute in Stewarton. This decided Cunninghame and his fellow teachers to leave the Kirk and form a Congregational

Church, for which he was elected pastor.[4] But the Presbytery of Irvine nominated another man to be minister. Cunninghame challenged this in court, and won. This brought the internal disagreements in the Church of Scotland to a head and is regarded as one of the main catalysts for the 1843 Disruption, when 474 ministers, sacrificing their houses and stipends, broke away from the Church of Scotland to form the Free Church.[5] The Congregational and Free churches had a significant influence on many individuals and events in this story, beginning with Elizabeth Oswald, a member of the Free Church and heir to the Oswald fortunes.

Elizabeth Oswald

On the death of Richard Alexander Oswald, the Scotstoun estate was inherited by his sister Elizabeth (1767–1864). Elizabeth was born, lived and died at Scotstoun. She was a generous hostess and had her portrait painted by the society artist John Graham Gilbert. Miss Elizabeth, who lived to the age of ninety-seven, may have attributed her robust physical and mental health to her renowned self-discipline

---

4. Congregationalist churches, while part of the Protestant tradition, are autonomous. Each congregation has the right to determine its own affairs and choose its own minister.
5. Another breakaway group formed the United Presbyterian church in 1847, which in 1900 merged with the Free Church to form the United Free Church. This body then reunited with the Church of Scotland in 1929, as the New Church of Scotland; Urquhart, *Along Great Western Road*, p. 118

and moderation. She certainly had energy, and at the age of eighty-four travelled to London for the Great Exhibition of 1851. Given her good health, or perhaps contributing to it, Elizabeth never consulted a doctor until she was ninety. She died in possession of all her faculties, busy with charitable and religious work almost to the end as, like many wealthy people in the Victorian age, she recognised that her happy financial situation brought with it an obligation to improve the lot of others. She was active and influential in the local community, and in 1848 she granted the Free Church land and non-financial assistance to build the Oswald School for the local mining community in Knightswood. In later years, fewer people worked in the mines, but adherents of the Free Church continued to send their children to the school. A decade later, members of the Free Church held services in the school and it was their internal disputes which eventually led to the birth of Anniesland Hall.

When Elizabeth died in 1864, there were no further siblings or direct male Oswald descendants to inherit the family fortune or to fly the evangelical flag. However, this banner had already been flourished vigorously by Robert Haldane, who had married Elizabeth's sister Catherine in 1785. When Elizabeth died, the Scotstoun estate and the vast wealth of the Oswalds were inherited by Robert and Catherine's grandson, James Farquhar Gordon Oswald, an evangelical and father of James William Gordon Oswald, who built and funded Anniesland Hall.

5. The Haldanes:
Authoritarian Evangelicals or Liberals?

The Haldanes had been barons in Perthshire since at least 1296, and Protestants before 1585. They never lacked the courage of their convictions and some members signed the Solemn League and Covenant opposing Oliver Cromwell. Subsequent Haldanes were members of parliament and friends or relatives of great and influential men. In 1759 Captain Robert Haldane MP of Gleneagles and Plean, 'an arrogant, ambitious, purse-proud man',[1] who had accumulated a huge fortune in the East India Company's Maritime Service,[2] bought the Airthrey estate near Stirling. When he died in 1768 the estate was inherited by his four-year-old great nephew, Robert Haldane.

Young Robert Haldane's widowed mother, from the devoutly Protestant Lundie family, made sure her children understood the importance of preparing their souls for eternity. She died when Robert was five and he, his brother James and their sister were brought up by their grandmother Lady Lundie, who provided

---
1. Namier and Brooke, *The History of Parliament*.
2. The East India Company's merchant fleet.

for their material and spiritual needs and introduced them to people who would further their educations and careers. Although receptive to religious teaching as a child, the teenage Robert abandoned his clerical aspirations and looked for adventure.

As noted in Chapter 2, while Catherine Haldane's great uncle, Richard of Auchincruive, was negotiating terms with the Founding Fathers, France and Spain seized the opportunity presented by Britain's diminished prestige and its preoccupation with events in America to try to regain territories, including Gibraltar. In 1780, seventeen-year-old Robert Haldane became an officer on HMS *Monarch*, commanded by his uncle and guardian, Admiral Duncan (1731–1804). In 1781 he transferred to the *Foudroyant*, an 80-gun warship which had been captured from the French at the Battle of Cartagena in 1758. The *Foudroyant*, commanded by Duncan's friend John Jervis, was regarded by some as the finest ship in the Royal Navy.[3]

In 1782 the French navy attempted to recapture territory in India. That April the British dispatched a squadron, led by the *Foudroyant*, to intercept French transport ships delivering supplies to their compatriots in the subcontinent. Near the French Channel Island of Ushant, the *Foudroyant* engaged with the largest French ship, the 1,778-ton *Pégase*. After a 45-minute battle, during which Robert Haldane ignored a warning from an old sailor that he was making himself a mark for the enemy, on the grounds that in the discharge of his duty 'he would disdain to think

---

3. A. Haldane, *Memoirs*, p. 29.

of personal danger',[4] the *Foudroyant* was victorious. Haldane, who spoke fluent French, was detailed to board the *Pégase* and bring its commander back to the *Foudroyant*. He performed this task with skill and courage, according to a report to Admiral Duncan from his captain, John Jervis.

The *Foudroyant* was involved in major engagements throughout the war and played a leading role in the relief of Gibraltar. In the face of the combined Spanish and French navies, a large British fleet was dispatched to carry troops and supplies to the besieged British forces. As Haldane later saw it, God was on his side: a tempest scattered the French and Spanish fleets, leaving Algeciras Bay virtually open; then the wind dropped and the enemy ships were becalmed. The British convoy, with an east wind behind them and the *Foudroyant* in the lead, sailed into Gibraltar, 'amidst the cheers and acclamations of the garrison'.[5]

Having witnessed numerous examples of Haldane's energy, character and courage, John Jervis, now Lord St Vincent, predicted a glorious naval career for him, but peace was signed in 1783 and Haldane retired from the navy at the ripe old age of 19. Two years later, Robert married Catherine Oswald. Her father, George Oswald, had inherited the Auchincruive estate from his uncle Richard of Auchincruive in 1784. George was already a wealthy man and the addition of Auchincruive made his seventeen-year-old daughter a significant heiress – although not at that

---

4. A. Haldane, p. 30.
5. A. Haldane, p. 34.

point the obvious heir to the entire Oswald fortune. The newly-weds settled at Airthrey, where their only child, Margaret, was born in 1787.

Haldane initially directed his energies to improving his estates, landscaping and planting trees. He created a 30-acre artificial lake and commissioned Robert Adam to design a castellated mansion and a romantic 'hermitage', ornamented with verses from Oliver Goldsmith's ballad *Edwin and Angelina.* In jest, Haldane advertised for a hermit to take up residence and then had to deal with several genuine applications. He balked at Adam's fee for building his mansion and brought in a cheaper contractor to execute Adam's design.

An eighteenth-century man of means like Haldane had ample time left over from walking his estates, managing his staff and experimenting with horticulture, arboriculture and architecture, to consider the philosophical issues of the day. Although he had fought gallantly against the French, he began to read deeply into the ideas underpinning the French revolution. While he soon distanced himself from Jacobin excesses, he questioned the merits of the war with France,[6] and the institution of slavery, writing in 1800 that 'a scene of melioration and improvement in the affairs of mankind seemed to open itself to my mind, which, I trusted, would speedily take place in the world, such as the universal abolition of slavery, of war, and of many other miseries'.[7] However, as a

---

6. Likewise, Lord St Vincent, who thought it 'unnecessary, impolitic and lamentable'.
7. A. Haldane, p. 84.

landowner who believed his wealth had been earned, he was disinclined to foment any revolution in his own backyard and looked instead at the wider world.

Haldane's wider world now encompassed the world to come. His brother James, also a naval officer, was profoundly influenced by the pastor of an Independent Congregation in the naval town of Gosport, Dr Bogue, whom he had met when he was fifteen. Dr Bogue prescribed books for James to read while he was at sea and both brothers visited the pastor when they were in port. The influence of their devout mother and grandmother eventually bore fruit and James and Robert became committed evangelical Christians around 1794. James Haldane travelled the country as a lay preacher, aided by distributing gospel tracts, later a significant element in Anniesland Hall's outreach programmes.[8]

In the nineteenth century, having decided that the Kirk expended insufficient energy on saving souls at home, let alone in 'all the world',[9] hundreds of people defected to the evangelical and congregational movements in which Protestants of various stripes united to preach the gospel. Many evangelicals, then and now, believe that the pronouncements of Old Testament prophets are simultaneously a validation of Jesus Christ the Messiah (as foretold in the Old Testament) and a prediction of both current events and the Last Judgement.[10] Texts in both Old and

---

8. A tract is a short political or religious pamphlet, handed out to members of the public.
9. Mark 16:15 'Go ye into all the world and preach the gospel to every creature.'
10. St Matthew's gospel is an early example of finding tenuous links

New Testaments are used to anticipate the Last Days. Happily for evangelicals, wars and rumours of war have always abounded, providing an urgent and perennial incentive to hector souls towards salvation.[11]

Nineteenth-century enthusiasts took advantage of merchant ships regularly plying the expanding empire to travel to the heathen nations, and redoubled their efforts to 'preach in all the world', thus consciously hastening the imminence of the Last Days. The Haldanes' mentor, Dr Bogue – 'whose thrilling appeal on behalf of the Heathen had before this time roused a missionary spirit in the country'[12] – was instrumental in establishing the British and Foreign Bible Society, the Religious Tract Society and the Missionary Society, founded in 1795. He was responsible for training missionaries for the Missionary Society, the most renowned of whom, David Livingstone, later benefited from the influence and support of Robert Haldane who, with his brother James, had joined the Society in 1795. Robert, the man of action, had found his cause. The 'young and ardent Enlightenment man' formed a desire to bring the souls of Africans and Indians to the Lord.[13]

---

from events in Jesus' life to statements in the Old Testament. Another example is the glorious aria in Handel's *Messiah*, 'I know that my redeemer liveth', where the words of Job, a nomad and farmer who lived around 1800 BC, are seen as prophesying the return of Jesus.
11. Matthew 24: 6-13 'And ye shall hear of wars and rumours of wars .. for nation shall rise against nation, and kingdom against kingdom: and there shall be famines, and pestilences, and earthquakes in diverse places… and this gospel .. shall be preached in all the world for a witness unto all nations; and then shall the end come.'
12. A. Haldane, p. 97.
13. A. Haldane, p. 97.

5. The Haldanes: Authoritarian Evangelicals or Liberals?

Despite his huge investment in Airthrey, Haldane decided to sell the estate and set up a mission in Bengal with the proceeds, but the East India Company refused permission. Although William Wilberforce had persuaded the House of Commons to pledge support in 1793 for 'the religious improvement of the natives' and to install schoolmasters and chaplains throughout India, Haldane's proposal came up against 'a dismal front of ghastly opposition'.[14] Haldane believed that the East India Company directors' stance was a reaction to his former sympathy with the French revolution, or their fear that Christianity might upend the caste system. This was not fantastical – until the end of the British Empire lower castes in India and Sri Lanka, and communities dominated by other tribal groups, such as the Malay, found that adherence to Christianity provided the networks and confidence they needed to rise in society. Haldane argued that rather than upsetting the peace in India, Christianity would lead to stability and to closer ties with Britain, citing as evidence that 'while the heathen slaves in the West Indies have united in insurrection, the converted Africans have continued peaceable and faithful',[15] but the Company was adamant. The plan was abandoned and Haldane focused his energies closer to home.

Robert became a director of the ecumenical British and Foreign Bible Society, whose mission still is to translate and distribute affordable bibles to people in all nations, and funded the Society for the

---

14. A. Haldane, p. 102.
15. Letter to Haldane's long-term acquaintance, the President of the Board of Control and Secretary of State for War, Henry Dundas ('Harry the 9th'), 21 September 1796.

Education of Africans. In 1799 this society brought twenty boys and four girls from Sierra Leone to be given a year's Christian education in Edinburgh. When the children first landed in England, they were housed in Clapham, under the care of the Clapham Sect.[16] They played in Wilberforce's garden with his children, even flogging his son when they were playing soldiers.[17] The daily roll call was not a simple matter due to their frequent, if temporary, disappearances. It transpired that the sons and daughters of African chieftains were such a curiosity that neighbours would bring them into their grand houses for a closer look. The innocent children were happy to be invited in, and were always returned unscathed. There was more to fear from disease, and several died. During a local outbreak of smallpox the children were inoculated and sent to St Pancras isolation hospital, which delayed their voyage to Edinburgh. While they were in St Pancras a rumbling feud between Haldane and the Clapham Sect's Zachary Macauley came to a head. Macauley objected to Haldane managing the Africans' education and Haldane, who was funding the entire enterprise, insisted on maintaining his authority. Haldane withdrew financial support and the children finished their education (a slightly more secular one than Haldane had planned) at the Clapham Sect's

---

16. A group of well-connected social reformers and abolitionists who met regularly between the 1780s and 1840s and campaigned successfully for various reforms. Members included MPs, a governor-general of India, influential churchmen, William Wilberforce and Granville Sharp. Despite the name, most of them were members of the Church of England.
17. Hague, *William Wilberforce*, p. 295.

African Academy in London and were then returned to Sierra Leone.

Haldane's dispute with Macauley was indicative of his character. He had strong views and the money to promote them, but the stronger his view, the more obdurate his intolerance of dissent. The Scottish churches had rejected the traditions and rituals of the Anglican Church and based their moral standpoint on their own interpretation of the scriptures. Like many evangelicals, Haldane formed his own version of cast-iron truths on the basis of his personal understanding of the Scriptures. As a wealthy man he was able to support and influence people who would promote his understanding of the Truth; like many powerful men, he surrounded himself less and less with people who disagreed with him.

In 1797 he and James set up the Society for the Propagation of the Gospel at Home (SPGH). The following year Robert sold Airthrey and his estate at Plean in Stirlingshire so that he could access £10,000 to build chapels, support missionaries and set up the Glasgow Tabernacle and other seminaries where young men were trained to become evangelists. Between 1798 and 1810 Robert donated over £70,000 to the SPGH and he and James built or purchased eighty-five churches in Scotland and Ireland.[18] In the Congregationalist tradition, these were officially autonomous, as new churches could decide on their own constitution and form, although

---

18. This introduced him to the Talbot Crosbie family. In 1885 Eugenie Diana, a member of the Talbot Crosbie family requested her new husband to build Anniesland Hall.

the authoritarian Robert frequently interfered in their religious practices. The churches flourished for a time, despite vociferous condemnation by the General Assembly of the Church of Scotland, but their success was short-lived. As Haldane's nephew Alexander pointed out, 'it was when opposition from without died away that the internal instability appeared'.[19]

Although Congregationalists generally practice infant baptism, the churches established by the Haldanes baptised by adult immersion, as did Anniesland Hall later.[20] Like the Brethren later, they broke bread every Sunday, rather than once a month. The brothers also supported exhortation, whereby any male member of the congregation could rise during weekday meetings and address the assembled company on some passage of Scripture. Recognising that exhortation threatened to undermine the authority of ordained ministers, Robert tried to prevent a dispute developing. In 1805 James ignited a heated debate by announcing that exhortation could take place on the Lord's Day, rather in weekday services, and that he (now a minister of a Congregational church) would no longer baptise children. James then attempted to calm matters, writing that 'if we are all acting on conviction, and both desiring to know the will of Jesus in this and in all other respects, I have no apprehension of disunion',[21] but he did not ask himself how he came to have exclusive access to the will of Jesus. Although

---

19. A. Haldane, p. 229.
20. This practice mirrored the experience of Jesus, who was baptised by John the Baptist. Brethren members tend to bristle when the christening of babies is described as 'baptism'.
21. A Haldane p. 229

5. The Haldanes: Authoritarian Evangelicals or Liberals?

both brothers declared that they regarded all believers as worshippers of God, they settled on the principle of 'union without compromise'.[22] There was a rupture with the Edinburgh Tabernacle, and a tussle over the Glasgow one. As in the case of the children from Sierra Leone, Robert Haldane would remove funding from organisations and individual preachers who did not bend to his will.[23]

The Continent was even more benighted than the Church of Scotland, so Robert and his wife embarked on a mission to France and Switzerland in 1816. They made their home in Geneva, the cradle of Calvinism but now a 'stronghold of Satan' where he reported that the theological students were 'involved in the most deplorable darkness' and knew more about heathen philosophers (Socrates and Plato) than the Gospel.[24] Evangelicalism was gaining ground in a Europe emerging from war and resentful of the duplicitous compromises the Church of Rome had made with Napoleon. Haldane's vision and leadership qualities attracted young men to the evangelical movement and, between 1816 and 1819, he inspired scores of them to spread the evangelical revival movement across Europe, as far as Italy and Hungary. Revivals gathered momentum in Germany, the Netherlands and France, where the number of French Protestant clergy more than doubled between 1829 and 1843.

His appetite for foreign adventure perhaps sated, Haldane returned to Scotland in 1819, residing

---
22. William Hague p.295
23. A. Haldane, p. 229.
24. A. Haldane, pp. 412–14.

in Edinburgh and at the Auchingray estate in Lanarkshire, which he had purchased in 1809.

He read widely and continued his passion for improving his estates, but at fifty-five was not ready to retire from the theological fray. Like William Cunninghame, Haldane was a man of his time, fascinated by new discoveries in the sciences and seeing them as tools to prove the literal truths of the Bible, rather than as evidence that perhaps some of the scriptures could be seen as poetry or myth.

He published *The Evidences and Authority of Divine Revelation* in 1816, a project he undertook because of the dim view he held of the calibre of existing works on the subject or, more particularly, of their authors. The respected scholar Bishop Warburton, for example, 'was a giant in learning, but his views of the Mosaic economy were sufficient to indicate his unsoundness'.[25]

Haldane was well on the road to believing that Almighty God could only be interpreted by the chosen, of whom he was chief. His intransigence led to an almost terminal schism in the British and Foreign Bible Society. The society had included the Apocrypha in the editions published for use on the Continent, on the grounds that the bibles would not otherwise be accepted in Catholic countries.[26] When

25. The Mosaic economy was a dispensation, a system of divine government suited to the needs of the Mosaic nation (mainly Jews and, for some specific laws, Christians). It was admired as it opposed idolatry and prescribed the worship of the one true God; A. Haldane, p. 384.
26. The Apocrypha consists of several books which are in the Greek Old Testament, but not the Hebrew scriptures. They are accepted as Holy Writ by the Catholic and Orthodox churches, but were removed

Haldane, with his customary vigour, investigated the authenticity of the Apocrypha, he concluded there was no place for it in the Society's bibles. This led to a huge controversy, with Haldane publishing numerous intemperate pamphlets over twenty years. Haldane prevailed, but most Scottish and some English branches left the society.[27]

Haldane's vision, once global and dynamic, was shrinking into a bitter splitting of hairs and personal attacks, which included falling out with William Wilberforce for consorting too much with ungodly men and worldly politicians in his efforts to form a coalition against slavery.[28] The rest of Haldane's life was spent producing booklets on abstruse theological issues and indulging his controlling nature, publishing his final work in the year of his death, 1842. He was buried in Glasgow Cathedral.

Robert Haldane's legacy can be seen through twenty-first century eyes as a shining example of Victorian religious philanthropy, partly lasting and inspiring, and partly of its time and best left there, such as: his obsessive and biased study of the scriptures; his equation of physical phenomena with spiritual truth; his arrogation to himself of the 'duty of exposing error, however harshly';[29] and his insistence that saving souls was of greater importance than improving social

by the Protestants at the Reformation.

27. The ex-naval officer could still fire shots across enemy bows. One of his pamphlets on the Apocrypha controversy was entitled *Exposure of the Rev. Henry Grey's personal misrepresentations, doctrinal heresies, and important misstatements, respecting the Bible Society, as contained in the letters of Anglicanus*, 1828.
28. A. Haldane, p. 564.
29. A. Haldane, p. 229.

conditions. Like many evangelicals, he believed that a saved soul would naturally prosper in this world as well as the next, whereas an unreconstructed sinner might misuse any material support offered by the well-meaning to fund the drinking, gambling or other vices inherent in his fallen state.[30] Many of Haldane's prescriptions for church services survived – adult baptism, breaking of bread (communion) every Lord's Day, and exhortation, where any man could rise as the Spirit led and share his insights with the congregation – and these formed the bedrock of Anniesland Hall.

Haldane was also a visionary, championing the spread of religion through ordinary men who had been trained as grassroots preachers, rather than as dictated by an overweening centralised and – as he saw it – corrupt organised Church. He offered encouragement and funding, but in theory let local circumstances influence practice on the ground. He donated vast sums of money without regard for political or commercial gain. He sympathised with the original impulses of the French Revolution and supported the cause of justice for all men of all nations. According to Haldane's nephew, the intelligence and demeanour of the African children he brought to England 'convinced Mr Pitt that the African race is not naturally inferior to the European' and strengthened the Prime Minister's support for the abolition of slavery.

---

30. For the Brethren and other evangelicals, people are 'saved' at a specific point in time when, having realised they are sinful and unable to help themselves ('lost'), they 'give their hearts to Jesus'. In doing this they trust Jesus to guide and support them, whatever their mistakes and the pitfalls along the way. Being saved is an act of humility and faith, and a commitment to follow Jesus henceforth.

Haldane's most visible legacy today is in the name of a modest street of three- and four- storey, cream sandstone flats that leads south from Glasgow's Victoria Park to Dumbarton Road by the river Clyde. As in so many streets in the area, the quality of the houses in Haldane Street declines the closer you get to the river – there is a villa at the north end overlooking the park, then apartment buildings with less generous proportions and ever more flats per landing as you move south. On the north side of the park, directly opposite, is a more well-to-do mirror image of Haldane Street, Airthrey Avenue, where my father Jack lived and died.

Given Robert Haldane's enthusiasm for saving the souls of Africans and Indians, it is ironic that his grandson, James Farquhar Gordon (later Gordon Oswald), was heir to both the slavery-based wealth of the Oswalds and the compensation paid in 1833 to Lady Lilias and Richard Alexander Oswald of Auchincruive.[31]

In 1804, Robert Haldane's seventeen-year-old daughter Margaret married James Farquhar Gordon, the couple thenceforth being known as Mr and Mrs Haldane Gordon. James Gordon had four children from his first wife Lilias, but it was his and Margaret's son James who, in 1864, took on the Oswald name and fortune and the Scotstoun estate.

---

31. <insert pic FN89, re compensation>; UCL website, Centre for the Study of Legacies of British Slavery, www.ucl.ac.uk.

6. The Oswalds in Scotstoun

Until the later twentieth century the Oswald estates in Scotstoun and Anniesland consisted of farmland with scattered mines and brickworks. As it ran from the river Clyde to the Forth and Clyde canal, to which Richard of Auchincruive had so presciently contributed funds (see Chapter 2), the bricks, coal and clay could easily be shipped in any direction. The brickworks used ironstone deposits and brickmaking material from an abandoned ironstone pit within the estate boundary and, with the Industrial Revolution at full throttle, profits from the ironstone works and the Skaterigg Brick and Tile Works, one of the biggest in the west of Scotland, added to the Oswald fortune.

Life for the Scotstoun miners, as for miners everywhere, was harsh. Their homes were poorly constructed, overcrowded and insanitary. By 1863, most of the buildings were of stone but, as they had no ceilings, their thatched roofs offered limited protection from rain and snow. Like his neighbour James Smith (whose father had bought the Jordanhill estate in 1800 and whose wealth also came from the West Indies trade), James Farquhar Gordon Oswald set about improving the physical environment for his workers and their womenfolk, who struggled to keep things clean. He built fourteen miners' cottages on the Crow Road, which had originally been a drove road from the West Highlands – 'crow' is a corruption of croadh, the Gaelic for cattle.[1] In 1869 Oswald added Skaterigg further along Crow Road. This was a settlement of twenty clean, tidy, well-constructed, two-room cottages, built of local bricks and grouped round a square. In the central area there were two wash houses with boilers, coal cellars, two wells with water brought directly from Loch Katrine and four closets 'erected where they are least offensive to sight and sense'.[2] Oswald was a benevolent landlord who ensured that rents were kept low and evictions unheard of. The cottagers could use the co-operative store, which yielded a members' dividend of two shillings in the pound.

The mines did well in the mid-nineteenth century. In the case of ironstone in particular, the Oswalds were again in the right place at the right time. Scottish pig iron had been unsuitable for wrought iron or steel, as its high phosphor content made it brittle when it cooled. In 1828 the Scot James Beaumont Nielsen patented his new hot blast process, which made the production of iron and steel from Scottish black band ironstone the most cost-effective in Britain. Ironstone, plentiful in Jordanhill and Scotstoun, is a hard rock which contains a high proportion of an

---

1. A drove road is a route for cattle drovers to bring livestock to market.
2. 'Notes of Miners Houses', *Glasgow Herald*, 14 January 1875.

iron compound. The ironstone in the Oswald estate was of such high quality that just over two tons of raw material could be smelted to give a ton of pure iron. Producers had a ready market in Glasgow as steelworks, shipyards and railway works flourished. By the latter half of the nineteenth century the city was a vibrant industrial, engineering and commercial centre attracting thousands of workers from Ireland and the Scottish Highlands, who increased the city's population from 77,000 in 1801 to 275,000 in 1841. Steel production in Scotland grew from 1,199 tons in 1873 to 58,500 tons in 1890. In the mid-nineteenth century more than half of British steel ships and a quarter of all the locomotives in the world were made in Glasgow, creating, despite periodic downturns, thousands of jobs in direct and ancillary trades.

As Richard of Auchincruive had so ably demonstrated, commercial success lies in: being in the right place at the right time; seizing the opportunity; and recognising when to pull out. Oswald could see that with the expansion of the city of Glasgow, selling the land itself would bring him better returns than his mines. Glasgow's growing population of skilled engineers and industrialists, the owners of factories, ships and shipyards, the bankers and professional classes, needed somewhere to live and play, and looked to the suburbs. The city's residential areas had been spreading westwards since the heyday of the Tobacco Lords.

Given the prevailing southwesterly winds, it made sense for those who could afford it to move west to escape Glasgow's noxious tanning and brewing industries, and the increasingly unsanitary maze of closes and wynds in the old city, where fifteen to twenty people often occupied a one-room flat. These slums were an ideal breeding ground for disease and gave rise to cholera epidemics in 1832 (when 3,000 people died in Glasgow alone), in 1848 and in 1853, by which time the City Fathers had understood the link between the filthy environment and disease and took decisive action. A complex system of tunnels, aqueducts and pumping stations opened in 1859 and still supplies Glasgow with fresh water from Loch Katrine, forty miles away. The City Fathers also acknowledged the need to improve housing and, in 1866, sent the City Improvement Trust to Paris to study Baron Haussmann's urban renewal programme. Under the 1866 City Improvement Act the trustees were responsible for purchasing and clearing the worst slums and adapting the traditional tenement design to provide cleaner, safer housing for thousands.[3] Following outbreaks of typhoid, minimum requirements for ventilation were imposed, including specified ceiling heights, tenement courtyards, and open closes front and rear for all but the wealthiest. Except for garden flats, which have their own entrances, traditional tenements are entered by a close that gives access to a common stairwell and the back court. Many of these common stairs feature beautiful wood and wrought-iron banisters, wally (porcelain)

---

[3]. The word 'tenement' is not a qualitative term, although some people imagine it denotes dirty, crowded living in Glasgow, but a legal term from the Latin 'tenere' – to hold. Property or land is owned by an overlord or the Crown and is 'held' by the tenants who pay feu or other duties. In Scotland, occupants can own their tenement flats, but have certain obligations, particularly in the common parts.

tiles which, after 1884, often had Art Nouveau dados, and stained-glass windows on each mezzanine level.[4]

With more people moving to the suburbs, public transport was booming. In 1836 James Oswald MP steered the New Anniesland Turnpike Act through parliament. It established that a turnpike road, now the A82, should run north west from St George's Cross in the centre of Glasgow, via Anniesland Toll, and follow Thomas Telford's route as far as Inverness.

Several developers, such as the Great Western Road Trustees and the Kelvinside Estate Company, subsidised frequent horse-bus and horse-drawn tram services along the Great Western Road to encourage speculators to buy or lease the land.[5] The Kelvinside Estate Company's pitch to building speculators claimed that 'the Public may build with confidence that full omnibus accommodation will be provided so as to render a residence on These Grounds every way suitable'.[6]

Residents of the West End suburbs and, from 1901, Anniesland, could now commute along the broad, straight road to the city. The Glasgow, Dumbarton and Helensburgh Railway, previously designed to carry freight to the Clyde ports, opened passenger stations at Jordanhill and Anniesland in 1886.

---

4. 'Wallies' was a Glasgow term for false teeth, while pairs of 'wally dugs' (pottery Staffordshire dogs) adorned many Glasgow mantelpieces.
5. The tolls were removed in 1882 and the last horse-drawn tram ran in 1902, by which time trams were electric and ran the length of Great Western Road to Anniesland Cross.
6. Quoted in Urquhart, p. 31.

6. The Oswalds in Scotstoun

Professional workers, previously confined in small insalubrious tenements, could now dream of spacious flats with indoor toilets, or stone villas with substantial gardens, all a short train ride from the city centre. Speculators bought plots near the railway stations and down Crow Road and built four-storey, red sandstone, mansion blocks grouped around back courts for hanging out the washing. Where the blocks fronted thoroughfares there were often shops and tea shops on the ground floor.

Numerous architects were involved in designing mansion blocks, villas, churches and swing parks.[7] The style and quality of the buildings varied, as can be seen most clearly in Partickhill, where streets begin at the top with imposing terraces, villas and blocks with one six-apartment flat per floor, and descend in altitude and quality to buildings with three flats on each floor sharing a toilet in the close, in some cases until the 1980s. One stipulation was that where a speculative development stopped abruptly, a link had to be left so that another building could be grafted on at a later date. There are still tenements with fireplace forms on the outside walls, sometimes because of this requirement, sometimes as a result of bomb damage.

The improved transport links to the city centre not only opened up the West End to speculators, but also to inspired planners and architects such as Alexander 'Greek' Thompson and George Gilbert Scott. Greek Thompson designed elegant terraces along Great

---

7. They fondly imagined that one swing park could service multiple blocks, forgetting the inherent tribalism of children, who saw off unauthorised interlopers from other blocks.

Western Road and villas on the side roads set out in leafy crescents and squares; Gilbert Scott created St Mary's Episcopal Cathedral on Great Western Road and the new Glasgow University buildings in Gilmorehill in 1870. Attracted by the university, academics and intellectuals joined the commercial elite to take up residence in Hyndland, Partickhill, Gilmorehill and Kelvinside, followed of course by schools, churches and leisure areas. This was, and still is, a lovely area of varied yet harmonious architectural styles, tree-lined streets, hills and squares where students, lecturers, literary types and professionals live. These neighbourhoods extended to the edge of the Oswald estates and, given the new transport links to the centre of Glasgow, Scotstoun and Anniesland were no longer rural communities.

As the mine deposits became exhausted – mining ceased in 1890 – and materials for the brickworks grew more expensive to source, James William Gordon Oswald saw that Scotstoun's fresh air and easy access to town were ideal for commuter communities and began feuing off land to developers in the late 1880s.[8]

This was an era when industrialists across Europe and North America took inspiration from Robert Owen, a draper, socialist, philanthropist and entrepreneur, who bought the New Lanark cotton mills from his father-in-law, the philanthropist David Dale, in 1799. Owen believed that ignorance and

---

8. The system of feuing, in which the purchaser/leaseholder of land for housing or commercial development had to pay an annual fee and other incidental duties to the original landowner, pushed up the price of building land to levels above those in England, with the exception of London.

immorality were not innate to workers, but were the result of unhealthy and brutal conditions. His vision was to create communities rather than just the bricks and mortar of factories and houses for those who toiled there. He treated his workers humanely, focusing in particular on children's welfare. The amenities Owen provided in New Lanark included a nursery school, an enlightened education (featuring dancing lessons) for older children, good quality housing, and a store that sold goods at reasonable prices while supervising purchases of alcohol – a forerunner of the Co-op system. Statesmen, reformers and businesspeople visited the mills, saw the social and commercial benefits of treating the workforce humanely, and sought to emulate Owen. These businessmen included the Oswalds and, from 1888 and on a more ambitious scale in Port Sunlight, William Lever 1st Viscount Leverhulme.

Like Leverhulme, James Farquhar Gordon Oswald aspired to create harmonious, productive communities, with (unlike the deist Owen) the church as the focal point. He built a recreational hall and houses for his estate workers to the south of Victoria Park in 1874, and granted land and £500 towards the construction of the Whiteinch United Free Church, completed in 1877. Like the Congregationalist Lord Leverhulme, who built churches of several denominations in Port Sunlight, the Oswalds showed some flexibility regarding denominations but they had to be broadly evangelical. Unlike the teetotal Lord Leverhulme, who held a referendum so his tenants could decide whether the 'dry' Bridge Inn in Port

Sunlight should have an alcohol licence, and accepted the affirmative result, James Farquhar Gordon Oswald was intransigent regarding the spiritual welfare of his workers and the people living on his estates, and built no pubs. When feuing off his land in the 1890s, Oswald stipulated there should be no trafficking or selling of liquor and no pawning, in perpetuity. This remains the case in Anniesland and Jordanhill, in that there are no pubs in the area, although in the 1990s a couple of restaurants appeared, selling drinks with what can loosely be termed 'meals'.

The Oswalds' powers were limited. A three-minute walk from Anniesland Hall, in the eastern shadow of the railway embankment, a huge art deco cinema was built in 1939. Opposite the cinema a roadhouse, the Esquire House, was built around 1962, its louche glamour cocking a snook at the shades of the Oswalds, whose writ had not run beyond the railway line.

The Glasgow Borough of Partick voted to lay out a public park to celebrate Queen Victoria's 1897 diamond jubilee and the Oswalds donated part of their estate to the borough for this purpose in 1886. In addition to creating what many believe is the prettiest park in Glasgow, with woods, lakes, islands, a bandstand and the Fossil Grove,[9] the creation of Victoria Park provided work for 1,000 unemployed shipbuilders. It also added significantly to the value of the surrounding streets of villas and terraces then under construction, particularly those on Oswald land.

---

9. A group of fossilised stumps and roots of eleven extinct trees which can be seen in situ, protected by a Victorian pavilion.

The Oswalds donated the miniature, four-dial, lamp post Clock Tower (now a Grade C listed building) which overlooks the boating pond and stands in line with Gordon Street,[10] which is parallel to Haldane Street, to the south of the park.[11] Oswald arranged for four plaques to be placed round the base of the clock, one of them reminding us that 'now is the day of salvation'.

Oswald was generous, but only to those he considered deserving. He left bequests to trusted servants, including 'to Margaret Murray of South Cottage Annan, long the faithful and valued maid of my said late wife, an annuity of fifty pounds'.[12] When he left an annuity of £300 to the Orphan Homes of Scotland at Bridge of Weir in Renfrewshire it was only for 'so long as these Homes are conducted on sound Christian principles and to my son's satisfaction'.[13]

The Oswalds were not present at the inauguration of their clock as the family was spending less time in Glasgow, preferring Brighton and Italy. It was to Italy that James William Gordon Oswald took his bride on

---

10. The name was changed to Inchlee Street in 1912 when Partick and other neighbouring boroughs were absorbed into the City of Glasgow. The names of streets already in Glasgow took precedence.
11. Minutes of The Partick Commissioners & Committees meeting with Mr Talbot Crosbie on 2 August 1887 to discuss details of the ornate clock tower.
12. His wife was Thomazine Crawford, mother of James William Gordon Oswald, who died in 1881.
13. Quarrier's aim was to remove poor orphan children from Glasgow's city streets. The homes were like villages, with a number of houses containing thirty or forty children and two house parents. The village included a school, church, infirmary, workshops and in one case a sailing ship cemented into the ground where a full-time sea captain taught the boys seafaring skills.

honeymoon, when the new Mrs Oswald requested that he build her a church as a wedding gift (see Chapter 1).

Oswald had chosen his bride well – she had a clear understanding of the duties of an evangelical Victorian millionaire. Her uncle, William Talbot Crosbie, had gone on preaching tours with Oswald's father in Italy. Talbot Crosbie, a wealthy deputy lieutenant and magistrate in County Kerry,[14] was a passionate evangeliser both at home and abroad, so much so that a visitor to his Ardfert Abbey estate observed that 'every Protestant in this village seems converted to God'.[15] William seems to have been more concerned with his tenants' souls than their material well-being. As 'Billy the Leveller' he greatly increased the value of his estates, but at the expense of his tenants. He improved the estate and put it on a sound financial footing (it had been deeply in debt when he inherited). When famine came, to avoid going back into debt he increased rents for his tenants, cleared land and demolished houses. 'The Attila of North Kerry was so notorious for his harsh measures during the Great Famine and for the number of people he evicted, that the Republicans took revenge in 1922 and burned Ardfert Abbey to the ground'.[16]

The estate passed to Lyndsey Talbot Crosbie in 1899. In contrast to his father, Lyndsey was known as the Emancipated Landlord. He sought the views of tenant and landlord representatives on land reform and managed to reconcile all parties, greatly

---

14. Deputy to the Lord Lieutenant, the monarch's representative in a county or area of similar size
15. O'Byrne, *Left Without a Handkerchief*, p. 64.
16. O'Byrne, *Left Without a Handkerchief*, p. 64.

facilitating the Land Conference of December 1902 and, ultimately, the Wyndham Act of 1903.[17] Initially a champion of moderate devolution, Talbot Crosbie increasingly supported Home Rule.

Lyndsey's energies were not directed exclusively at Irish matters. He was an active and innovative factor for the Oswalds in Scotland. The Talbot Crosbies already had connections in the area. Lyndsey's elder brother John, who had been disinherited, reportedly for marrying without his parents' approval, was a successful industrialist in Scotland and, for a time, owned a twenty-five per cent stake in the fiercely Protestant Glasgow Rangers football club. John was appointed manager of the Scotstoun Estate Building Company and worked closely with Lyndsey in constructing houses for the workers on Oswald lands.

Oswald and Lyndsey Talbot Crosbie considered Eugenie's honeymoon request. The perfect solution for a man who wished to serve the Lord while husbanding his God-granted wealth was to build Anniesland Mansions and Anniesland Hall. The men identified a plot of land on Great Western Road as an ideal location: shops and businesses in the development could serve the growing residential areas; commuters had easy access by bus, tram or train to the west of Scotland and to Glasgow city centre.

The Hall Oswald built would later be home to a group of Christians who yearned for a true community of believers – the Plymouth Brethren.

---

17. Under the 1903 Land Act, better known as the Wyndham Land Act, generous inducements would be offered to landlords to persuade them to sell their estates and transfer ownership to the occupying tenants.

Part Two

Blood of the Lamb I wish ye were whisky,
   blood of the Lamb, och aye!
Blood of the Lamb I wish ye were whisky –
   I wid drink ye dry!

(to the tune of *Campbelltown Loch*)

7. The Brethren

When I was ten my mother bought me a pair of gloves for Christmas. They were navy-blue leather and lighter-blue suede inside. They were dainty, elegant and more beautiful than the gloves my friend Barbara wore. A few nights later I dreamt that Jesus came back in a bus to take all the Hall members to heaven. The bus was ready and everyone else was on board, but just as I was climbing in I realised I had forgotten my blue leather gloves. I ran back to retrieve them and the bus drove away, leaving me behind. I woke and screamed in terror for my mother, who hurried in to comfort me, but I did not dare tell her the content of the dream – I knew even then that the sin of pride would lead to my perdition.

Like many dissenting movements, the Brethren were the fruit of soul-searching among 'men of good position and repute'.[1] These men felt that the established churches had diverged significantly from the practices of the New Testament church. From

---
1. Beattie, *Brethren*, p. 16.

beginnings in Plymouth and Dublin among affluent disaffected Anglicans in the early nineteenth century, the group built up networks of devout middle-class people who met in private homes to study the Bible. They concluded that when groups of believers became too formalised, established dogmas and built specific places of worship, they grew stale and ceased to search diligently for the guidance of the Holy Spirit. Foremost among them was John Nelson (J.N.) Darby, an ordained priest in the Church of Ireland.[2] Darby declared that 'he is an enemy of the work of the Spirit of God who seeks the interests of any particular denomination'.[3] If there was no denomination and no creed, there would remain only the Word of God, so it followed that the Plymouth Brethren should not be, and indeed never did become, a denomination.[4]

The problem that remained was how to determine what the Holy Spirit intended, as we have seen with the Haldane brothers (see Chapter 5). Under Darby's definition of an enemy of the work of the Spirit of God, conviction precluded compromise. Most Brethren assemblies had started life as splinter groups from more established churches, setting a precedent of

2. His uncle had served with Lord Nelson at the Battle of the Nile, hence his middle name.
3. Beattie, p. 14.
4. A distinction which is difficult for some to grasp. On 5 February 2022 an article in *The Times* was predicated on the supposed existence of a sect with a worldwide leader, but it has long been accepted that the Brethren are not a definable sect. As early as 1926, the United States Census of Religious Bodies stated, 'The body classified as Plymouth Brethren disclaim any designation whatever save those that the Scriptures apply to all believers as Christians. To accept any specific title would imply that they are a sect which they deny, sects or divisions being condemned in 1 Corinthians 1:10-15.'

secession from the outset, and sects and schisms were and are part of the movement's 'creative destruction'. In 1848 Darby had broken with what is now known as the Open Brethren to form his own sect; in 1850 the assembly in Hereford split over whether the Sunday evening service should take the form of an edifying address to believers, or a gospel mission to the unsaved – the option of holding each type of service on alternate Sunday evenings seems not to have been explored. Men with strong opinions believed that compromise was a dilution of God's will and any contrary argument made them more entrenched in their views and more convinced of their monopoly of the truth.

There had been evangelical revivals in Scotland in the 1620s and in the eighteenth century, and the Methodists in particular had spearheaded nonconformism, both religious and political, but it was the nineteenth-century Awakenings that were the genesis of Anniesland Hall. Society in Scotland, as in Western Europe and the United States, was changing. Instead of generations of the same family working together on their farms, and meeting and trading with their immediate neighbours, men and younger people moved to the industrial towns, stretching or breaking ties with their extended families and their home churches. Itinerant lay preachers stepped in, holding open-air rallies or meetings in secular buildings. Charismatic evangelicals claimed certainty in a rapidly changing world and the new close-knit communities formed by religious groups became a substitute for the families the migrants had left behind

In 1857, downcast by a recession, thousands of working men in New York attended prayer meetings led by a Dutch Reformed lay preacher, Jeremiah Lanphier. Their enthusiasm added momentum to the existing evangelical revival and over a million Americans were saved between 1857 and 1859. The evangelical movement spread to Ulster in 1859 and thence to Ireland and Scotland. Robert Haldane's system of training itinerant preachers worked in the Revival's favour as, although the Haldanes and their descendants did not formally join the Brethren, they sympathised with their religious activism and quest for absolute scriptural truth, and the men they trained could spread the Brethren message. Following the 1859 Revival, the Brethren and other dissenting movements received a huge influx of Scottish and Ulster working-class souls.

It is unsurprising that the dissenting churches, including the Brethren, appealed to the working classes. The established churches mirrored the structure of society and their doctrine was decided by Convocation in England (Canterbury and York) and by the General Assembly in Scotland. The clergy were set apart from their parishioners: physically, in the pulpit, from which an aloof cleric could pontificate to the congregation; and in appearance, in their clerical robes. Social strata were maintained among the parishioners as rich members could pay for separate family pews and distance themselves from the less wealthy.[5] A perception of venality was reinforced by the obligation on parishioners to pay tithes and pew

---

5. See Chapter 2 for description of Oswald's church at Auchincruive.

rents, a burden that weighed disproportionately on the poor.

There were no pew rents in Brethren assemblies. Initially, Brethren meetings had been in people's front parlours and the revivalist movement held rallies in open fields. Even when converts became too numerous to gather in private homes yet needed shelter from the elements, the premises dissenters rented, purchased or built were modest buildings where all could join together to worship, in free and unallocated seats. As the emphasis was on seeking eternal truths in the scriptures rather than on following prescribed rituals, the insights of lay preachers or simple members of the congregation had equal value, and the collective study of the Bible was a voyage of discovery all members could make together.

The established churches had tended to focus on maintaining stability based on centuries of tradition and, in several denominations (barring deliberate defection or apostasy) an assured progression for the faithful from infant baptism to eternal light. By contrast, evangelicals in the revivalist movement focused on evil within and without in a wicked world getting wickeder, and the constant threat of eternal damnation which, given the imminence of the Second Coming, loomed on the horizon. The remedy was not passive attendance at services and partaking of communion; the situation demanded immediate, decisive action in a conscious conversion (some assemblies still require the specific date when a soul had been saved), a daily battle against our inherently sinful nature, and an urgent imperative to save souls from the encroaching fires of hell. It called for mental strength, persistence and a determination to face down the forces of evil. Amid social upheaval in the cities and industrial towns this was a muscular faith, rooted in certainty, an inspiration to working men struggling against the dislocation and powerlessness the new industrial order was inflicting on them.

This is not to say that the Brethren were a politically radical movement. As firm believers in the imminence of the Second Coming, some assemblies opposed any involvement in politics, including voting in parliamentary elections, arguing that it diverted energy from the task of saving souls. Methodist, Quaker and Unitarian practitioners of the Social Gospel focused on social problems and supported trade unions and labour reforms.[6] Whereas, until the Second World War, the majority of Scottish Brethren members – skilled industrial and agricultural workers, miners and fishermen – were socially conservative. In the secular communities that had formed them, too much individualism was discouraged as it would upset the equilibrium of the group. Cohesion provided security. In their new spiritual home, such men continued to believe in submission to authority. They opposed membership of trade unions, the temperance movement and other community organisations since, while they shared the general nonconformist desire for working people to have a better life, they believed it should come through self-improvement, acquiring respectability and leading a regulated, disciplined and

---

6. These tended to be postmillennialist, believing that the Second Coming will not happen until social evils are eradicated.

alcohol-free life. Salvation was the only solution to social problems.[7] Only through casting sin aside could a man achieve the self-discipline, responsibility and prudence that would bring him health and material well-being.

As James Haldane had written (see Chapter 5), Christians would act in unison if they based their convictions on the will of Jesus. While James and his brother had engaged with evangelical organisations of various hues, albeit while carrying on disputes with a number of them, some assemblies decided that the will of Jesus was withdrawal from the world rather than co-operation. Having seceded from doctrinally prescriptive churches, the Brethren were, in general, unwilling to defer to any centralised arbiter of doctrine, and each assembly had leeway in its interpretation of biblical texts. Literacy was becoming more widespread throughout the nineteenth century, and members were able to identify the will of Jesus through prayerful and diligent study of the scriptures. Yet, however fervently the seekers prayed for humility and longed for a sign of divine guidance, the views of the strongest men in each assembly were the most likely to prevail.

While some assemblies held bible studies with Christians from other evangelical groups and welcomed them to break bread or preach at outreach meetings, others denounced these practices. By the 1870s, some of the Presbyterian churches were becoming more liberal and a number of them became hostile to the absolutist Brethren who then felt

---

7. Dickson, *Brethren in Scotland*, p. 301.

obliged to defend their turf against error from within and pressure from without. As Neil Dickson put it in his study of the Brethren 'the concept of a faultless, entirely sufficient Bible encouraged the Brethren to seek the perfect ecclesiology in scripture and to see other denominations as sinful for not accepting it'.[8] A besieged minority, they had to raise the drawbridge and guard, in particular, against wolves in sheep's clothing who could appear to share an assembly's beliefs while subtly undermining its foundations.[9]

Separation from other sects and organisations freed each assembly to focus on saving souls and removed the risk of contamination, of dilution – and of distraction, which they imagined afflicted the socially reforming evangelicals. The quest for purity led to internal ruptures too and by 1894 there had been seventy schisms in the Scottish assemblies.[10] Brethren membership grew throughout the nineteenth century, then strongly between 1921 and the Second World War, yet numbers were less important to some assemblies than purity. Many had been called, but few chosen. God did not desire vast armies, lest the believers vaunt themselves against Him.[11] Brethren pride in their purity would at least prevent the sin of pride in their numbers.

---

8. Ecclesiology is theology as applied to the nature and structure of the Christian church; Anniesland Hall, 'History of A Hall'.
9. Matthew 7:15 'Beware of false prophets, which come to you in sheep's clothing, but inwardly they are ravening wolves.'
10. Dickson, p. 168.
11. Judges 7:2 'And the Lord said unto Gideon, The people that are with thee are too many for me to give the Midianites into their hands, lest Israel vaunt themselves against me, saying, Mine own hand hath saved me.'

On the other hand, the numbers to be saved did matter – while the saints were shut in with Jesus, the restless world warred below and Evil in its many forms stalked the land.[12] The Brethren had deep roots in revivalism and were aware of Jesus' express command that they bring sinners to repentance. For some, this did mean co-operating with other evangelical churches to organise revival meetings. Many of the assemblies who chose to support the gospel crusades of Dwight L. Moody, the renowned American evangelist, benefited from numerous new recruits.

In 1873, 1881 and 1891, Moody toured all the main cities in Britain, attracting hundreds of thousands of people, including Queen Victoria and Prime Minister William Gladstone, to his rallies. These novel and uplifting spectacles led by a citizen of the thrusting New World were far removed from the grim preaching and prohibition of instrumental accompaniment to hymns and psalms which marked many Scottish church services. Moody's partner, the singer and songwriter Ira D. Sankey, heightened the excitement and the emotional impact of the events with his simple, vibrant 'human hymns', written in the style of the popular music of the time. *Sankey's Sacred Songs and Solos,* a collection of rousing and emotive hymns authored by a range of men and women, was first published in 1873. Its final 1907 edition comprised 1,200 hymns, 200 by Sankey himself, and is still used at many gospel services today.

---

12. 'Shut in with thee, far, far above the restless world that wars below', *The Believers Hymnbook* (1885), no. 129.

Moody preached in various locations in Glasgow, most famously in 1874, in the newly opened Kibble Palace, a vast glasshouse in the Botanic Gardens on Great Western Road. It was estimated that 6,000 people gathered inside the Palace, with a further 15,000–30,000 outside.

Although he was a Congregationalist, Moody broke bread with the Plymouth Brethren while he was in Glasgow. Whereas the Brethren and many Nonconformists focused their preaching on the minutiae of the scriptures, Moody took a more human perspective. He was a storyteller. He quoted unrelated verses from the Bible which served his purpose, then developed his theme, using everyday language that ordinary people could understand. He seemed to speak directly to each individual in his audience, manual worker or middle-class professional, drawing them in with the simplicity of his message and the emotional power of Sankey's music. Thousands were saved and flocked to the dissenting churches. In the Anniesland area, the question was how to accommodate them; as several times before, the evangelicals turned to the Oswald.

In the early nineteenth century there was no local dissenting church in the Oswald lands, which were still largely rural. At the time, Knightswood was part of Renfrewshire, in the Presbytery of Paisley. People wanting to attend services in Renfrew had to take the ferry across the Clyde – churchgoers were exempt from the halfpenny fare. They walked barefoot to save precious shoe leather and put their shoes on for the last yards leading up to the church. As noted in Chapter

3, in 1848 Miss Elizabeth Oswald granted land and funds in Knightswood for a school, which was attended mainly by adherents of the Free Church. From around 1850, the headmaster held gospel meetings in the school, which attracted enough people to form a small congregation. Numbers swelled in 1854, after Renfrew Free Church organised an outreach in the area. The members pooled their resources and built their own church in 1858, adjacent to the school in what is now Academy Park, across Knightswood Road from the current Knightswood School. This church, standing as it did on the top of a hill, was called Hillhead Church (not to be confused with Hillhead Church on Observatory Road in Kelvinside).

Within a year of the foundation of West Hillhead Church, there was a schism. Members who felt the first minister was not a man with a message for the people, left the church and resumed meetings in the school. In 1865 a man with a message did appear, Duncan Matheson, a celebrated evangelist who had preached to soldiers during the Crimean war and distributed bibles in the Crimea and in Sardinia. He too had been inspired by the 1859 Revival and ran a short gospel campaign, which resulted in the formation of the evangelical West Hillhead Christian Association in March 1865. The minister and elders of Hillhead Church decided, as noted in their minutes, that the meetings in the school 'tended to perpetuate a state of matters discreditable to the sacred cause of religion' and took control of the Oswald School in 1867, banning all Association activities.[13]

---

13. Anniesland Hall anniversary leaflet

It was time, once again, to appeal to the Oswalds. James Farquhar Gordon Oswald advised the Association to hold open-air meetings and kitchen meetings while he built them a hall. Construction went on apace and on 5 January 1868 the first Anniesland Hall, still within the Free Church, was opened on the north side of Anniesland Toll. This congregation, now known as the Anniesland Christian Association, and affiliated with the Glasgow United Evangelistic Association (GUEA), originally a working class organisation, briefly reunited with Hillhead Church, but in 1881 they split again.[14] The GUEA held a tent campaign on the west side of Crow Road (now Glasgow High School playing fields). Impressed by the numbers saved, among them pit workers who then returned so many tools they had stolen from the pits that they became an embarrassment to their employers,[15] Oswald withdrew permission for the Free Church to meet in the hall at Anniesland and granted its use to the Association, funding its pastors for over fifty years.

When Oswald married Eugenie her honeymoon request for a church (see Chapter 1) was timely. Glasgow was expanding westwards along Great Western Road, increasing Anniesland's commercial potential, and a development which included a church was a sound spiritual and economic decision. With the support of Lyndsey Talbot Crosbie the Oswalds

---

14. Due to subsidence, Hillhead Free Church later moved to Woodend Drive in Jordanhill. By that time, the Church of Scotland and the Free Church had reunited at least twice – in 1900 and 1929 – and it is now Jordanhill Parish Church.

15. Moss and Russell, *Range and Vision*, p. 67.

built a block of balconied red sandstone mansion flats on the south side of Great Western Road, the east side of Crow Road and the west side of Ancaster Drive.[16] This created a C-shape, sheltering an open space at the back of the buildings in which Oswald built what was to become the second Anniesland Hall. A single block in the same style was built on the north side of Great Western Road. As there were no buildings on the west side of Crow Road, the Oswald buildings towered incongruously over neighbouring structures, resulting in a wind tunnel from the west and the impression that one had reached the end of the known world; a passing aviator would have seen no other residential buildings of this height until he landed in New York. On the ground floor of the buildings on Great Western Road and the top of Crow Road banks, shops and tea shops formed a thriving community, attracting tenants and guaranteeing rental income for Oswald from businesses and residents.

---

16. The term mansion flats was coined in the late 1800s to describe blocks of apartments built with aspiring middle-class commuters in mind. The prefix 'mansion' was added to suggest a touch of class.

8. Anniesland Mansions

Serious thought had gone into the construction of the flats at 1597 and 1605 Great Western Road, which flanked the entrance to Anniesland Hall. The common parts were more generously proportioned and more expensively constructed than those of the other closes in the block. The polished terrazzo-floored stairs and landings were wide, with white tiled walls and green dadoes. Light flooded in from the glazed roof above.

The tenants of 1597 and 1605 enjoyed spacious, elegant but spartan living conditions. Each dwelling had heavy mahogany doors with leaded glass panels of stained glass, and in front of them, the customary wooden storm doors to defend against winter weather, although when Jack closed our storm doors at 9.30 every evening, it seemed more like he was reinforcing his defences against a hostile world. The rooms in the flats were high-ceilinged, with tiny ineffective fireplaces fed by coal which had been lugged up the stairs by alarmingly sooty coalmen and deposited in the coal bunker. The men then went back to their lorries and filled the street with their cry of 'cooooal'.

8. Anniesland Mansions

The view from windows to the back of the flat was blocked either by the flat opposite or by the vast grey bulk of the Big Hall roof, so Oswald had the rear external walls covered in white glazed bricks to reflect maximum daylight. Unlike the flats in the rest of the block, which had large kitchens (many still with ranges in the 1980s), 1597 and 1605 Great Western Road had 'kitchenettes' which were about eight feet by five feet and had a window looking out on the white tiled walls of the corresponding flat, twelve feet away. Parallel to the kitchenette was the maid's room, the same proportions as the kitchen, and so small it could fit into the other bedrooms three times. After maids no longer featured in ordinary households, in many flats the two rooms were combined to create a slightly larger H-shaped kitchen which was both cramped and difficult to clean. Because the Big Hall occupied the area which would, as in neighbouring closes, have served as a back court and drying green, 1597 and 1605 had access to the flat roof, where the children could play together and form lasting friendships – Barbara, who lived in 1597, has been a faithful friend for nearly seventy years. More practically, tenants could use the boilers, tubs and wringers in the well-appointed washhouse and hang out the washing in the breeze while we children marvelled at dead pigeons in the water tanks and, when unobserved, climbed outside the railings to drop moss and gravel on to policemen eighty feet below.

A more innocent pleasure was to greet bridal couples after their wedding ceremony in the Hall. Friday evening at 5.30 p.m. was the time for weddings, so that the newly-weds could spend the weekend together before going back to work on Monday. This was a great event for the children who lived in the flats around the Hall. After Friday tea we would hang around the entrance, along with the other bystanders attracted by the wedding car parked at the kerb, and scramble for the pennies the groom scattered as he and his bride emerged from the church.[1] The lives of the tenants and the life of the Hall were intertwined.

For it should not be imagined that Oswald had neglected God while pandering to Mammon. The centre of the ground floor facade of Anniesland Mansions was occupied not by commercial premises but by an imposing granite-columned portico which led into the Hall at the back of the block. This church was so effectively hidden from public view that in the 1930s the elders decided that the style and opulence of the structure should be utterly vulgarised by a giant red neon sign proclaiming 'CHRIST DIED FOR OUR SINS'. It was this building which became known as Anniesland Hall.

The Hall was an integral part of the mansion flats and shops, architecturally and financially, as it benefited from rents from many of the commercial properties, but its internal architecture was considerably grander than that of the shops and flats. Large but relatively low-ceilinged meeting rooms ran either side of a wide terrazzo-floored hallway, which led deep under the

---

[1]. A similar custom persisted at least until 1989 when passers-by in Partick tossed coins – pound coins – into our new baby's pram. A comfortably-off couple encroaching on a downtrodden area, we were too surprised at this spontaneous generosity to come up with a suitably gracious response.

flats until opening out into the Big Hall. This was a splendid vaulted auditorium seating 800 people. Its roof rose in the centre of the surrounding flats. There are no pulpits in assembly halls as speakers preach from platforms. In the apse of the Big Hall there were two platforms, the lower of which could be pushed back inside the high platform to reveal a baptismal tank large enough to accommodate full adult immersion.

The fittings of the Hall were of top-quality materials. Floors were wooden or terrazzo, as appropriate, with walls tiled or wainscoted. Benches were of oak. It was on one of these oak benches that in 1925 Jackie Jackson sat alongside his friends Donald McLean and Lachlan McNair, when all three gave their hearts to Jesus.[2]

There was a large kitchen, three 'side halls', and passageways winding under the tiered seating in the Big Hall which led to more small rooms, as well as a discreet passage which led directly to the hallkeeper's first-floor flat at 1597 Great Western Road. In addition, one flat on the first floor of 1605 was reserved for missionaries to stay rent-free when they were home on furlough.[3] The other flats in these two closes were occupied by trustee-approved tenants, including several Brethren families. As the rest of the block was sold off over time, the Trustees retained

---

2. When the Hall benches were replaced by individual chairs Jack salvaged several benches and used them as bookshelves in his front room. The wood was of excellent quality and was put to good use, bearing bibles, books by the delightfully named Baptist writer F.W. Boreham, and the *Rubáiyát of Omar Khayyám*, which Jack had bought in Egypt.
3. Home on leave, which usually lasted for up to a year.

1597 and 1605 so they had some control over the behaviour of tenants living directly over the Hall. The Trustees were entitled to the feu duties and rents for these flats, paid to the factor who came round every month to check the meters and collect the cash.

This church began as an independent mission hall. Oswald appointed the GUEA's existing pastor, Malcolm Ferguson, to lead the congregation in the new building. Ferguson, a former steelworker, was pastor at Anniesland from 1899 to 1934, and is revered to this day. He combined eloquence, robustness and humanity. Long after his death, stories were told of his common touch. When a housekeeper said she could not attend his service because she had to have the house ready for her master's return, Ferguson rolled up his sleeves and helped with the chores. The woman was then able to attend the service. When a man threatened to throw him down the stairs, the burly pastor called his bluff, earning the man's respect. Ferguson did not pull his punches in his sermons either. As later Hall members noted approvingly, 'he spoke of sin and judgment with tremendous feeling and his audience saw his face go grey and solemn as he spoke of the lot of the unregenerate.'[4] More than this, he emphasised the love of God. This was a man for his time when, in both the infant Labour movement and in the evangelical churches, there was room for thoughtful debate, soaring oratory and a desire to raise up the common people. The evangelical and labour movements grew in tandem, searching for truths and committed to improving the material or spiritual

---

4. Anniesland Hall anniversary leaflet

well-being of working-class folk. The Hall continued to function after Ferguson's death, but Oswald died in 1937 and the establishment became a burden to his widow. In 1942 Anniesland Hall was given to the congregation, whose leaders were becoming convinced that it was God's will that they should cease being a subsidiary of the GUEA and become an independent body, part of the Brethren movement.

Letter from Lachlan McNair to Sub-lieutenant J. Jackson, E. Engineering Officer, HMS *Glengyle*, 1st February 1942:

> Dear Jackie
> First of all there are some Hall happenings of great importance for the future, and of special interest to you. Mrs G.O. who is elderly and rumoured to be not quite herself, … has signed a proper legal document handing over the Hall and adjoining property to three men as Trustees … – all members of Brethren Assemblies. … It looks as if the Lord is about to answer our regular prayer, that Anniesland Hall might be blessed and made a blessing and that the Lord might have His own way there. …
> So you're on another ship. I hope you haven't allowed the other to go to Davie Jones' locker. Any prospect of a home port soon? …
> Mr McNeill mentioned at the meeting this morning that he had had a phone call from G.I.S. who said they had just had a letter

> from George by which they learned that he had had a narrow escape. Practically all his equipment was lost and had he been a minute later in the morning he would have been obliterated too. He was thanking God for answered prayer. No other details were given, but it looks like George was in the thick of it.
>
> We have increased our family recently by the addition of five hens. They were six originally but one died. However we are getting three fresh eggs per day. We got less than three foreign eggs in three months from the Co-op. The last three they gave us, Anne let them fall swinging the bag round her head. She's as wild as ever.
>
> Jean joins me in sending our warmest Christian love and greetings,
> Lachlan

Like most of Britain, Glaswegians led a double life in the Second World War, continuing to work, worship and play in the midst of food rationing, bombs aimed at the shipyards but frequently destroying nearby housing, and constant anxiety over the fate of loved ones overseas. Any information sent to and from forces personnel had to be carefully worded, and as bad news from the front was at least partly censored, people became adept at reading between the lines. Lachlan McNair's guess that Jackie's ship, HMS *Breconshire*, had been sunk was incorrect, but not far out. Seven weeks after he wrote this letter the vessel was seriously damaged by Axis bombers while carrying fuel and high explosives to Malta and sank on 27 March. Jack was not on board, having already been transferred to the *Breconshire*'s sister ship and escort, HMS *Glengyle*.

The news from Lachlan was indeed of special interest to Jack. That Jack, an electrician and son of a cabinet maker, should be part of a group taking over the management of the Anniesland property is testament to either the power of the Lord to 'have His own way' or to social mobility in twentieth-century Scotland.

Blood of the Lamb

2. Anniesland in 1936 showing a Gospel Tent

3. Anniesland Hall

9. The Jacksons

Jack was born in 1916 into a large, close and boisterous family, with three surviving older sisters and numerous cousins. His mother, Rebecca, was from Tarbert, a fishing village on the Mull of Kintyre. His father John's family came from Ayrshire and, before that, Ireland. Jack (John Black Jackson) had the good fortune to be born to a father who was earning a steady wage and, as part of the category of engineers, miners and shipyard workers, was exempt from conscription in the Great War.

The Jacksons occupied a two-apartment flat in Sawmill Street in Partick, across the road from the Clyde shipyards where John Jackson worked as a carpenter.[1] John's contribution to the war effort included constructing combat aeroplanes, which at the outset of hostilities consisted of wooden trusses with fabric laid over them and glued in position. A skilled and versatile craftsman, John Jackson found employment in a variety of industries over the years: he worked on the fit-out of the *Queen Mary*, the magnificent ocean liner which was launched at John Browns yard

---

1. In Scotland, flats are described in terms of 'apartments' – the number of rooms excepting the bathroom or kitchen. In any case, at the time when Jack was born the toilet was in the close and there was no bathroom.

in 1934; he benefited from the construction boom in the thirties when he did the woodwork on sandstone terraced houses in the Scotstoun estate. Young Jack would bring John his 'piece' [sandwich] at midday, little guessing that nearly fifty years later he himself would buy one of these terraced houses on Airthrey Avenue and furnish it with the round rosewood card table and standard lamp his father had crafted and given to Jack and his bride as a wedding gift.

When Jack's little brother, William Ralston Jackson, the fifth surviving child, was born in 1922 the Sawmill Street flat no longer met the family's needs and five years later they moved to Archerhill Road in the new garden suburb at Knightswood, formerly part of the Oswald estate, which had extended west as far as Knightswood and north of the Great Western Road.

It is said that Knightswood and neighbouring Temple were named after the Knights Templar. At his 1128 meeting in Scotland with the Grand Master Hugues de Payens, a cousin or close connection of St Bernard of Clairvaux, King David I granted the Order land in Midlothian and at Abbotsinch in Renfrew, a parish close to Knightswood.[2] The land changed hands several times over the centuries and, by the nineteenth century, most of it was a combination of farmland and ironstone mines – the latter owned by the Oswald and Smith families.

After the First World War, to acknowledge the debt the country owed to the millions of working-class men who had fought in its defence, Lloyd George's

---

2. Abbotsinch meant abbot's island and is now the name of Glasgow's airport, which occupies most of the site.

coalition government passed the Housing and Town Planning Act of 1919 to encourage local councils to provide 'homes fit for heroes'.

Another motivation was to head off civil unrest. Glasgow people had staged rent strikes in 1915, and in 1919 tanks were stationed in the city to deter striking engineering, shipyard and mine workers who had gathered in George Square. The tanks were not deployed, but there were violent clashes with the police.

Alarmed at the poor physical condition of many working-class recruits during the war, and wary of Bolshevism's potential for tapping into the disgruntlement of returning soldiers, the government provided subsidies to local authorities so they could build 500,000 houses within three years.

Glasgow Corporation purchased land in various parts of the city for housing schemes, the largest of which was Knightswood, where construction began in 1923 on a garden suburb with 7,000 homes for artisans and their families. The most typical dwellings were two-storey, four-in-a-block, 'cottage' style houses with gardens. Unlike Drumchapel, which came later, Knightswood had schools, sports grounds, shops, a hospital and eight churches. It also had a sense of its history, as some of the new streets were inspired by Sir Walter Scott's *Tales of the Crusaders* – Athelstane Road, Talisman Road, Kestrel Road.

Knightswood was the ideal environment for an aspiring working-class family on a reasonable income and the Jackson children flourished. All were well spoken and literate, with the rumbustious wit that comes from being part of a large family. They were gregarious, good-looking and keen to earn their way in the world. Jack passed his eleven-plus exam and was accepted at the local senior secondary school, while his sisters, Annie, Rena and May (respectively ten, eight and six years older than Jack), obtained clerical posts.

In later years, Jack and his older sisters enjoyed recalling their friends and their scrapes from Sawmill Street. One of Jack's favourite expressions was 'the ba's on the slates!' meaning 'it's all over!', referring to the abrupt end of a street football match whenever the ball ended up on a tenement roof. In contrast, they were largely silent on life in Knightswood. This was possibly because community life in a garden suburb was less intense than in a street of tenements, or possibly because a shadow passed over the Knightswood house.

In 1930, when Jack was fourteen and Willie eight, their mother died. Her daughters later speculated that she had suffered from breast cancer but, in the manner of the day, medical information on such an intimate subject had not been shared with the children. All they knew was that Rebecca had been admitted to hospital for an operation and died four weeks later. Jack kept a diary at the time and on the day of his mother's death noted, 'Mother died'. Five days later his diary entry read, 'Mother's funeral. Flowers lovely.' The matter-of-fact entries masked internal devastation. Jack had adored his mother, going without school dinners so he could buy her a birthday present, and rushing home from school so that he could help her with the chores. Now she was gone. While Annie, Rena and May did their best to support their younger brothers, and certainly took care of their material needs, the sisters were considerably older than Jack, and Willie was too young to provide any emotional support – but Jack drew strength from Anniesland Hall.

Led by Pastor Ferguson, the Hall folk became Jack's family, his vocation, his social life and his intellectual stimulus. Whenever tragedy struck one of their own, the members moved with speed and compassion, discreetly providing practical support and spiritual sustenance. They opened their hearts to Jack. It was at this time that Jack's relationship with Donald McLean and Lachlan McNair grew the deep roots that sustained it for over seventy years as the church became a Brethren assembly and flourished, then fell asunder.

Willie, only eight when his mother died, relied on his older sisters to be mother substitutes, and on Jack. The girls were growing into womanhood and embarking on their careers, and with Annie already courting, John Jackson remarried. Until the marriage, his bride Mary was housekeeper to the renowned entertainer and songwriter Sir Harry Lauder, who presented the newly weds with a set of crystal glasses and a decanter. Lauder, whose compositions included *I Love a Lassie* and *Roamin' in the Gloamin'* [twilight], had at one time been the highest-paid performer in the world, a favourite of Churchill and Queen Elizabeth the Queen Mother.[3] Mary did not neglect

---

3. The song, covered in 1965 by Bing Crosby, remained part of Scottish consciousness. In 1973, when I worked briefly at the Long John whisky bottling plant, the forklift truck driver was a Polish refugee called Roman. An accomplished seducer, he was known as Roman in the Gloamin'. I was not allowed to tell my grandmother where I was working.

to flaunt her connections. Her stepchildren wearied of her tales of the great and the good who had enjoyed her hospitality, and loathed her airs and graces and her cat, which she wore like a fur collar round the house. When on floor-polishing duties May would rub the floors furiously in the hope that Mary would slip and break her neck or the cat's or, preferably, both. The ploy failed, but from the day Mary died the cat, by accident or design, was never seen again.

Jack and Willie were close, playing chess and football together, collecting cigarette cards and going to the football. They loved the cinema matinees where all the children would cry 'Mind yer back!' whenever a baddie crept up behind the goodie – a practice Jack continued throughout his life when watching films on television (by then it had been revealed to him that physical attendance at the cinema was a besetting sin). Coach travel was cheap and the brothers often went walking on the nearby Campsie Fells, or took the train to visit their numerous Beggs cousins in Ardrossan on the Ayrshire coast.

The boys' uncle, Jonny Beggs (1879–1969) was a prominent figure in Ardrossan. An evangelical member of St John's Church of Scotland (originally a Free Church) he, like Jack later, became involved in Christian outreach work, and was Sunday School Superintendent for many years. Uncle Jonny's interests were wide. From 1947 to 1950 he was on the committee of the Ayrshire Archaeological & Natural History Society at the same time as Ayrshire's adopted son, Dwight D. Eisenhower, was Honorary President.

He was Provost of Ardrossan from 1949 to 1952.[4] In February 1952 one particularly poignant duty for Provost Beggs was to deal with the aftermath of a fire in a Glasgow Corporation home for convalescent children in Ardrossan, which killed six boys aged between eight and ten. Beggs Terrace, an unprepossessing street in a 1950s housing estate, was named in his honour.

Uncle Jonny's evangelicalism and social commitment made him a potent role model for his extended family. The young Jacksons remained particularly close to his youngest daughter Ruby (1920–2014). Lively, intelligent and ambitious, Ruby worked as a secretary in London before training to be a speech therapist, then going on to be Vice Principal of a Dublin College. After the Church of Scotland decided to ordain women ministers in 1969 Ruby saw that a career in the Church would satisfy her Christian calling and her adventurous spirit, and in 1981 she became minister of St Bride's Church in Callander, Perthshire. At the age of 66 she got married for the first time, to Leo, who, to the stupefaction of the family, whisked her off to honeymoon in America on the Cunard liner *Queen Elizabeth 2*. It was a long way from Ardrossan, but not too far from the story of many Scots who have long looked across the Atlantic for the fulfilment of their dreams.

Ruby was one of many Scots who made the most of their capabilities. Opportunities for bright young men, and some women, abounded in early twentieth-century Glasgow. The great leap forward of the Scottish Enlightenment had retained much

---

4. The equivalent of a mayor in England.

of its momentum and Glasgow University awarded degrees in law, medicine, civil service, teaching and divinity. Smaller but growing numbers of students enrolled to study science and engineering, which became specialties of the Royal Technical College, later Strathclyde University. Many Scots benefited from experience in the forces and the colonies where, at a young age, they had been given the authority and opportunity to experiment in civil and military engineering and in management techniques. Some emigrated to Canada, widening their horizons and sending back to Scotland news of the advances they had encountered in the New World. Glasgow was confident and booming, considered by many to be the Second City of the Empire.

This was the time when the professions in much of Britain were professionalised, opening up a white-collar career path for young men who might not have family connections, but who had the brains and the drive to succeed. Night school was the route to success for many, who could earn to support their families by day and study in the evening. Decades later, whenever my brother and I failed to display sufficient gratitude for our life of privilege and ease, we were reminded that Uncle Lachlan had sat at the top of a ladder under the skylight so that he could study by the light of the moon. His moonlit studies paid off as Lachlan became a Chartered Accountant and drove a Jaguar, while Donald McLean ended up as Glasgow manager of the Bank of Scotland. As Hall members they were not outliers – another elder, Harold Reid, the son of a shipbuilder's clerk, became partner in a major Glasgow law firm. Jack, though intelligent and articulate, lacked the confidence to join any of the major professions but satisfied his natural curiosity and love of language with excruciating puns and intense study of the Bible. Aware that no talents should be unused, Jack was active as a Sunday School teacher, a youth leader and a lay preacher – a leader of young folk, if not yet of men.

Jack obtained his school leaving certificate and in 1931 was taken on as an apprentice electrician at Barr & Stroud, an optical engineering firm which had moved to a new purpose-built factory at Anniesland Cross in 1904.

The company was in the forefront of developing optics for scientific and military use and had been designing rangefinders for the Admiralty since 1891. They were perfectly placed to benefit from the pre-1914 arms race, when Britain and Germany were rapidly expanding their navies and vying with each other for technological dominance. Japan was a major customer and source of endorsement, as its naval experts confirmed that 'Barr & Stroud rangefinders had played a major part in the Japanese victory' at the Battle of Tsushima during the 1904 Russo-Japanese war.[5] Admiral Togo visited the Anniesland factory in 1911, and several pairs of Japanese workers spent extended periods there learning to adjust and repair rangefinders, with an inspector, Mr Yamada, even setting up an office in Anniesland. As an illustration of the fickle fortunes of war, another Japanese visitor was Isoroku Yamamoto, later Commander-in-Chief

---
5. Moss & Russell p. 55

of the Combined Japanese Fleet which attacked Pearl Harbour in 1941. Supping with potential devils required a very long spoon, as Barr & Stroud discovered when two employees were sent to set up subsidiaries in Austro-Hungary, then the First World War broke out and the Scots were interned for the duration of the conflict.[6] But, in general, war was good for business. During the Great War, in addition to their existing optics lines, the company developed fire-control systems and parts for submarines and surface ships. Demand for their products and their capacity for constant adaption and design improvement ushered in a boom in profits and jobs in Barr & Stroud for the duration of the war.

When the First World War ended there was a surfeit of military equipment across the globe, and orders for new rangefinders were drying up. As a result of this and the depression in general, Barr & Stroud nearly foundered, but the British military became concerned that the primacy in the production of binoculars enjoyed by Zeiss, the German optical instrument manufacture, could cause problems in any future conflict.[7] To counter this, Barr & Stroud began producing the binoculars which are still prized today.[8]

By the time Jack joined the firm it was a major player in the optics market, working closely with Glasgow University to maintain its technical lead for

---

6. Moss and Russell, pp. 136–7.
7. Zeiss developed a well-regarded rangefinder but, being stereoscopic, it could be affected by the weather, or the health or mental state of the operator, or simply by the stress of battle. Barr & Stroud's rangefinders were more reliable.
8. To mark Barr & Stroud's 100th anniversary, the company sent Jack a pair of binoculars in a leather case, even though he had left the firm nearly forty years before.

decades.[9] In this lively and competitive atmosphere Jack was a skilled tradesman rather than a technical expert. He had the intelligence to match the students and researchers from the university, but his background meant their world was closed to him. Jack's experience at Barr & Stroud deepened both his inferiority complex and his determination to improve his own prospects and those of his children and his nephew.

By the early 1930s, rearmament had restored Barr & Stroud's fortunes. The advent of radar had greatly reduced demand from the Navy for rangefinders, but submarine periscopes, field rangefinders and gunsights were needed in quantity. Unbeknown to Jack, in 1938 the Nazi High Command had identified Barr & Stroud and the neighbouring gasworks as potential targets and had sent an aircraft to take aerial photographs of Anniesland.

What Jack may also not have known is that Barr & Stroud had been brought to the attention of William Joyce, the Irish-American fascist known as Lord Haw-Haw, who broadcast Nazi propaganda to Britain each day. He was reported to have boasted that German bombers would destroy 'that little toyshop in Anniesland'. The hi-tech response to this threat was to paint crude black windows on the blank brick wall of the factory to confuse the Luftwaffe in the 1940s – and which bemused me twenty years later – and to decide on a contingency plan for resisting a German incursion into the factory. As the company had only five First World War rifles at its disposal, the Deputy Chairman

---

9. Between 1958 and 1963 Barr & Stroud built the first computer in Scotland.

Dr James French sent a proposal to the Secretary of the Ministry of Aircraft Production. 'We have suggested …. the establishment of a Pepper Corps, and we have actually laid in a stock of pepper.'[10] Bags would be made available on the routes to the entrances most likely to be used and employees trained to hurl the condiment at the invaders. Dr French had thought this through carefully, taking advice on whether the allocated employees would have to be enrolled in a combat corps under the terms of the Geneva Convention. They concluded 'that as they are not attempting to take life it is unnecessary to do so'.[11]

Like many large companies, Barr & Stroud was a meeting place for young men and women, several of whom were members of the nearby Hall and remained Jack's close friends all his life. One precision engineer, Archie aka Gary Walker, was Jack's best man, and several others were engineers or secretaries in the factory. They and other Hall young folk would spend free days together, taking an early bus to the coast or the train to Loch Lomond where they could spend the day hillwalking, then return to the shore to sing choruses round a camp fire. Since it stays light until eleven on summer evenings, decorum could be observed, with everyone back in Glasgow before dark.

Jack was a natural sportsman and there were plenty of companions to form a football team or to play tennis in summer in Victoria Park. As Brethren assemblies flourished across Glasgow, tournaments were set up between the Halls – an opportunity to

---

10. Moss & Russell p. 137
11. Moss & Russell p. 137

improve physical fitness and marriage prospects. Witty, good-looking and employed, Jack was an excellent catch and caught the eye of several young women, but he was choosy.

War broke out in 1939. As part of their principle of separatism, Brethren were often pacifists, and as an employee in a reserved occupation Jack was exempt from conscription. Nevertheless, in the first week of hostilities he enlisted in the navy and served in all the main naval theatres of war. He was assigned to the 9,776 ton MV *Breconshire*, originally a cargo liner.[12] She had been modified as an auxiliary supply ship to carry fuel oil, operating mainly between Alexandria and Malta. Naval ships docked in Malta for repairs and used the island as a starting point for sorties against Axis fleets, so it was essential to maintain supplies to Malta, which has very few natural resources. The Axis powers were aware of this and fighters patrolled the sky so they could torpedo any Allied vessels. The ships, if spotted, were sitting ducks.

Originally, the Italians were the main threat, but accounts of the time indicate little hatred from their prey. In order to hit the target, planes had to fly low and drop their bombs with precision near the vessels, eliciting admiration for their courage. The pilots flew so close to the ships that the sailors could see the expression on their faces, making it all too easy for them to imagine the Italians' mothers, as anxious and grief-stricken as their own.[13] The fellow-feeling

---

12. A type of merchant ship which carried general cargo and often passengers.
13. 'To be truthful, I felt sorry for him and I thought of his mother.' Quoted in Thomas, *Malta Convoys*, p. 185.

was no doubt helped by the fact that Italian planes and accuracy (or motivation?) were inferior to the Germans' and when he saw planes approaching, Jack would pray fervently that they were Italian, rather than German. Later on, the planes and pilots were all German, and the fight became more bitter, but many sailors retained their respect for their opponents, young men like themselves.[14] Never far from the shores of enemy-occupied territory, the men were allowed no more than four hours' sleep at a time. When they were awake they had to keep a constant lookout for submarines and bombers. It was difficult to be certain whether a dark shape in the water was a large fish or a torpedo. Torpedoes in the Second World War could travel at 50 knots (26 m/s) for more than 10,000 yards (9,000 metres), but a skilled ship's pilot could take avoiding action to evade an oncoming missile. It was a great relief for sailors to join a ship with crew known for their prowess in swerving when a torpedo was powering towards them.

The North Atlantic, where Jack's ship escorted convoys, was a different story. He described life there as 'part boredom, part terror'. For weeks they saw nothing but grey sea, which could be hiding any number of U-boats. Sinking ships were far from any source of help. If you fell or jumped from a ship in the Mediterranean, you had some chance of survival; in the North Atlantic you had none.

Throughout his life Jack rarely spoke of his wartime experiences, and then only following a

---

14. 'I have a vivid recollection of the pilot's white face staring straight ahead …. He was a brave man.' Quoted in Thomas, p. 111.

9. The Jacksons

trigger: while visiting me in Sri Lanka he recalled organising a football match at Trincomalee; and when the family went on holiday to Cornwall and the bright sunlight set off the skin condition which led to him losing an eye, he gave us young children a graphic account of Hiroshima, where he had been at the time of the Japanese surrender. When, on a family trip to Helensburgh on the Clyde, we saw the sinister bulk of a nuclear submarine emerging from the grey waters, Jack suddenly described the time he witnessed a Free French ship sinking with all hands. The order had been given to batten down the hatches and Jack watched helplessly as the Free French screamed from the portholes. He also recalled seeing sailors burn to death in oily waters after another sinking. My mother always forbade Bill and me to ask any questions – by then, Jack was often afraid to go to sleep and have his dreams peopled by eternally screaming sailors.

The war years were not good to the Jacksons. Annie's husband died of tuberculosis, leaving her alone in Leeds with a young son and, in those days before the Welfare State, no means of support. Jack made every effort to help her, visiting her whenever his ship docked at Liverpool. As a serviceman Jack had certain perks. He was given a seat at Anfield to watch Liverpool play and had a permit to travel from Liverpool to Glasgow. Leave was a joy, especially if Willie was also home from the air force, and Jack could recharge his spiritual batteries with the folks at the Hall. But leave could also be emotionally damaging – men who finally got more than four hours' sleep a night suddenly had the mental space to process the horrors they had not had time to deal with while they were at sea. Jack always left Glasgow without letting family or friends know when he was going back to his ship, but it is unlikely his loved ones failed to recognise the dark signs of his imminent return to war.

Service in the armed forces brought together men from all classes and walks of life. Jack valued the spiritual and temporal support provided by the global Brethren community. One of his most joyous moments was when he was able to meet up with George Stewart in the Middle East. For the rest of his life Jack made an exception to his instinctive sarcasm about the other men in the Hall, feeling George was 'douce',[15] and always spoke of him with loving kindness. George himself had a close shave, as Lachlan mentioned obliquely in his letter of 1 February 1942.

When Jack was wounded in the foot near Singapore he was invalided out to Adelaide, Australia. This was the land of his dreams. The Brethren there welcomed him and in that new world he was free from anxiety about his social status, so much so that when he was next in Britain he went to Australia House on the Strand to apply to emigrate to Tasmania. Inconveniently, it was a public holiday, Australia House was closed, and Jack never saw Australia again. Instead, he was sent to Japan for the final days of the Pacific war. He returned home with a Japanese sword which he may, as a sub-lieutenant, have been given by his Japanese opposite number, or he may have

---

15. One of many Scottish words deriving from French. Ina, from the east coast, would use 'I doubt' in the French way, meaning 'I suspect', and 'how d'ye cry it?'

purchased it. Whatever its provenance, we children regarded it with awe and reverence, convinced that if we even looked at the curved blade – revealed only when a secret button on the scabbard had been pressed – we would be cut to pieces. When Jack was eighty-two an 'antiques dealer' persuaded him that if the house was burgled Jack might seize the sword, wound or kill the intruder and stand trial for assault or murder, and bought the precious memento for £30. Jack's other souvenirs – a cigarette lighter made from an artillery shell case (nobody smoked), medals, ebony elephant bookends – remain in the family.

Jack's other war legacy was a deep admiration for officers who had attended naval college or public school. As a Temporary Gentleman (non-commissioned officer) he observed how these men could assume command and act authoritatively and decisively. Always uncertain of his worth, Jack longed for such calm self-belief, which in the war years often meant the difference between life and death. Throughout his life, Jack's tribal contempt for the ruling classes wrestled with his admiration for their leadership qualities and their easy assurance.

In 1944, when his ship docked in Birkenhead, Jack met up with Willie, who seemed distracted and unwilling to talk about the future. He had flown twenty-four missions as a flight engineer in a Lancaster, already well exceeding the average survival rate. The brothers parted, Willie returning to his base in East Anglia and Jack going to Glasgow. In January 1945 the Jacksons received the telegram every family dreaded. Their baby, their charming, sweet boy was dead. He was twenty. Just before take-off, his Lancaster had been sent a recall instruction due to poor weather conditions, but failed to receive it. The plane tried to gain height but spun into the ground near Barnham in Suffolk. Jack returned home to wait for Willie's body to arrive. He sat up all night by the coffin, clutching a chisel. When the day dawned he decided not to prise open the lid, fearing the sight of his little brother's mangled remains, or a bag of sand demonstrating that the body had been too badly damaged even to go in a coffin. Willie was buried, with due honours, in Renfrew. His name is inscribed in the great books of remembrance in Edinburgh Castle and St Clement Danes in the Strand. Jack took us to read Willie's name in these books, in beautiful script on huge thick pages. On all the family mantelpieces stood a black and white photograph of Uncle-Willie-who-died-in-the-war, an old man (it seemed to us children) with an air force side cap at a jaunty angle and a shy smile[16]. For Jack, the certainty of a lifetime enveloped in Jesus' love and hope of an eternity resting in His bosom could never lighten the weight of a brother's grief.

Age and the loss of his son weakened Jack's father, and Jack now bore most of the responsibility for his sisters, two still unmarried and one widowed with a young son. After he was finally demobbed, Barr & Stroud offered him a permanent commission as an electrical engineer but he turned it down. He was unemployed for over a year, then opportunity beckoned.

---

16. When my son was twenty-four I realised that he looked exactly like Willie. Only then did the full tragedy hit me – Willie had not been an old man at all. He had died when he was four years younger than my son.

Britain had limped out of the Second World War into a new world where its houses were in ruins and its factories had been turned to rubble. The United States was now the pre-eminent power and Britain, as the US Secretary of State Dean Acheson later said, had not yet found a new role. With the end of the war effort, demand for Britain's heavy industries, for ships, aircraft, munitions and Barr & Stroud's products, would plummet at the same time as competition from other countries began to rise.

To survive, the nation had to adapt and reconfigure for the future, which required an educated, nimble workforce; yet, like everything else, schooling had suffered in the war. More than 20,000 teachers had been called up and thousands of city children had been evacuated to the country, where the rolls were doubled to the point that half the pupils were taught in the morning and the other half in the afternoon. The disruption had adversely affected the education of children and the training of teachers.

Even before the war ended, the government had been planning a reorganised education system. The McNair report of May 1944 concluded that 'it would be of immense advantage to the schools if there were more who, before they became teachers, had experienced life in some capacity other than that of full-time students. It is to be hoped that this variety will be achieved in the immediate post-war years by the recruitment of men and women demobilised from the Forces and Auxiliary Services'.[17] Of course, the recruits had to be of good character, and a rigorous

---

17. The McNair Report (1944) Teachers and Youth Leaders, para. 78.

selection process would be applied, but for ex-service people aged between twenty-one and fifty who had served at least one year in the armed forces or in a war industry, no specific academic qualifications were needed. Unlike school leavers, who undertook three years' training, people from industry or the forces would receive one year's training with a two-year probation period, and earn an annual salary of £415 at a time when the average national wage was £350.

In general, teaching is the profession of choice for aspiring children of working-class parents, and Jack, who throughout his life had a burning desire to serve, was no exception. The McNair scheme was ideal for him, and with his experience as a Sunday School teacher and youth leader he was ideal for it. Even better, Jack would not have to travel far for his training. In 1913 the Smith family had sold the Jordanhill Estate to Glasgow Corporation and, after a hiatus during the First World War, an elegant red sandstone teacher-training college was completed in 1921 to serve students from across Scotland. The early cohorts consisted of people from all age groups, and from all backgrounds, from the tenements of Glasgow to the Western Isles – and Grangemouth.

Nessie

In Grangemouth, an industrial town near Edinburgh dominated by its docks, ICI and a huge BP oil refinery, a young woman was pondering her options. Agnes Leitch was the only child of Charles and Ina Leitch.

9. The Jacksons

A 'lad o' pairts'[18] born in 1896, Charles Alexander Leitch had not gone to university, but studied hard at night school and, after war service in the Middle East, found work at the BP refinery in Grangemouth. Small and outwardly unassuming, he was ambitious and spent several years with the BP in Persia before returning as a manager at Grangemouth. Charles was a member of the Plymouth Brethren in his quiet way – he was never one to declaim in the morning meeting, or to go out preaching, except in the local borstal. As a talented musician who had written several pieces, he put his musical gifts in service of the assembly. He acted as precentor in the morning meeting, as the organ, pummelled lustily in the Gospel Service on Sunday evenings, was considered inappropriate for the Breaking of Bread. Charles sang the opening notes of each hymn to set the right pitch for the congregation to join their clear, high, east coast voices in praise of the Lord.

Ina, properly Jemima McKee, was the second youngest of a family of twelve from Dalmellington, a weaving and mining village in Ayrshire. Ina was vague about the reasons, which may have included bullying, but before she was ten she went to live with her sister Aggie and the latter's miner husband in Tarbrax, a small shale-mining village in East Lothian, whose population has now dwindled to 200 souls. While coalminers were dirty and drank, shale miners were clean and god-fearing, or so Ina maintained. Tarbrax was isolated and exposed. One winter the snows were

---

18. A lad o' pairts is a youth, particularly one from a humble background, who is considered talented or promising

so severe and persistent that Ina and her friends built an igloo which they moved furniture into and played in for weeks. In 1925 Ina moved in with an aunt in Portobello, a charming seaside town on the Firth of Forth. Socially, this was a step up, as the aunt, a member of the Plymouth Brethren, lived in a solid stone villa overlooking the beach. Aged nineteen, Ina became a shop manageress and, a year later, the bride of Charles Leitch, fourteen years her senior. Charlie could be considered an excellent catch as a manager with prospects and sufficient income to buy a car in the 1930s. He was a quiet, dapper gentleman, utterly devoted to his lass, but Ina knew her worth and refused to marry him if he returned to work in Persia. Charlie, deeply smitten, agreed to stay. He was in love with his lass all the days of his life.

Unlike many newly weds in the 1920s, the Leitches were able to set up home in a BP manager's house embellished with silver coffee pots, condiment sets and other ornaments Charlie had brought back from the Middle East.

The BP was an old-fashioned, patriarchal employer. Grangemouth is on flat ground and, between the docks and the refinery, the company laid out wide, straight streets with semi-detached houses, much in the style of many Scottish council houses, for the workers and their families. There was a co-op and other small shops, but no churches or schools. There was no need for a pub or café as the workers could take their meals in the works canteen even after they retired, and the BP was not about to encourage consumption of alcohol.

9. The Jacksons

Further away from the refinery gates the houses became slightly bigger and better appointed and it was in one of these, a two-storey, semi-detached house, that the newly weds made their home. This home, and the bungalow they moved into later, was Ina's castle, always comfortable and warm, with tasty Scottish meals and plentiful supplies of homemade cakes and shortbread for the many guests she welcomed to her table.

During the Second World War there was a sharp decline in this abundance, potentially life-threatening for Charles and Ina's beloved only child. Agnes, or Nessie, was all that a doting father could wish for – musical like himself, obedient, Christian, a talented artist and needlewoman and devoted to her father – but she was a sickly child. She needed nourishment that the ration cards could not cater for, but Charles and Ina did not pray to the Lord in vain. Their friends the Galbraiths ran Upper Kinneil farm at Bo'Ness, close to Grangemouth – and incidentally where James Watt, observing steam from a kettle raising its lid, began experimenting with his steam engine. The Galbraiths were able to provide additional eggs for Nessie, and Ina no doubt drew the same demarcation lines between herself and evil black marketeers as she had between shale and coal miners. They were not so lucky with clothing coupons. Charles went without a coat one bitterly cold winter so that his daughter could have a warm new one, but this was the winter she spent almost entirely in bed and when she revived in spring she had outgrown the garment she had never worn. The sight of her father rubbing his hands as he went out in the cold haunted Nessie for the rest her life, although it is unlikely that he gave it a thought.

Eggs seem to loom large in memories of the war.[19] A Russian soldier, recognisable despite the lack of snow on his boots, was billeted with the family.[20] As a great sacrifice Ina offered him an egg and asked how he would like it. 'In a glass' was the response, to lasting hilarity in the family. In any case, they all survived, warmed by coal provided by the Lord who diverted German bombs aimed at the refinery so that they landed in sands of the Forth, sending up showers of coal. The same Lord who, in his mercy, diverted German bombs from the house of Charles' brother in Kent so that they landed on the Catholic school next door – or so Ina claimed.

Quiet but sociable, Nessie did not neglect her lessons at the local high school and attained excellent grades, giving her the choice between the Glasgow School of Art, Edinburgh University and Jordanhill Teacher Training College in Glasgow. 'Choice' is a relative term as neither parent would have been thrilled at their daughter associating with the bohemians at art school, and Ina was not convinced of the value to a girl of a university degree. Primary school teaching was an eminently suitable vocation for a young Christian

---

19. Woodrow Wyatt recalled that when the vegetarian cabinet minister Sir Stafford Cripps was invited to lunch at Buckingham Palace, Princesses Elizabeth and Margaret 'watched with horror and fury as Stafford polished off their egg ration for the week'.
20. In the First World War, a rumour spread across the United Kingdom that Russian soldiers – identified by the 'snow on their boots' – had landed in Scotland en route to the Western Front.

woman. She would have some influence on children's spiritual welfare and her artistic talents would be put to good use for school arts and crafts. On the other hand, Glasgow was a rough city, replete with strange men, and forty miles away. It was agreed that Nessie would not board in the city, but that her father would drive her to Falkirk every morning so that she could catch the Glasgow train. The precautions were in vain. After a hard winter when standing around on railway platforms again threatened Nessie's health, her parents decided she should, after all, board in Glasgow from Monday to Friday. She could now attend weekday evening meetings at Anniesland Hall.

Nessie excelled at her studies and collected a group of friends, particularly members of the Hall. She was pretty, talented, generous and naïve. She had been brought up an only child in a loving, comfortable home, in a small, close-knit community in a small town. Although she had friends outside the Meeting she had been enveloped in the Brethren's tight embrace all her life. Jackie Jackson was everything that her family was not, but he was still a member of the Assembly. Nessie, outwardly so meek, could not resist the charms of a man with life experience vastly more varied and hard-edged than her own. Jack courted her assiduously, buying her a box of sweets every week (she did not have the heart to tell him she did not like them) and taking her out to dinner at the Ivy Restaurant in Glasgow city centre, the height of sophistication. These dinners must have been a considerable sacrifice for Jack, who always regarded food as fuel and never lingered at the table, but they had the desired effect and eventually he was able to ask Charles Alexander Leitch for his daughter's hand in marriage. What a disappointment for Ina, just as she was becoming aware of the disadvantages of marriage to a man 14 years older than herself, Nessie was embarking on the same primrose path, and with a sometimes crude man from a lower social stratum and a lower income than her own gentle father. On the plus side, he was a member of the Plymouth Brethren. So, in July 1952 Charles and Ina laid on a wedding in Grangemouth, attended by numerous Christians and Jack's family. Jack's father came, with his wife Mary draped in a fox. The loud and lively Jackson clan were intimidating to Nessie, and objects of polite condescension from the mother of the bride.

After a two-week honeymoon riding a motorbike and sidecar through the western isles, the young couple returned to their new home in Anniesland Mansions. They were fortunate to be able to rent their own home in the early 1950s, a two-bedroom flat on the second floor of 1605 Great Western Road. It had easy access by public transport to city schools and the city centre, and a full range of shops just down the stairs. It was a cold, comfortless place, a far cry from Nessie's cosy home in Grangemouth, but she had made her marriage vows and she had a teaching career to look forward to, a ready-made community in Anniesland Hall, and a husband who was handsome, devoted to her – and fun. Jack now had his helpmeet and he and his bride could throw themselves into a life of service as active members of the Hall.

9. The Jacksons

4. Jack and Willie

5. Jack and Nessie's wedding, with Ina looking grand in fur (in July)

10. Fellowship

There were many meetings every week in Anniesland Hall, six on Sundays alone: the morning prayer meeting; the breaking of bread; Bible Class; Sunday School; the evening prayer meeting; the gospel service. It was not for the faint-hearted, but made it considerably easier to keep the Sabbath holy as it left little time for the temptations of watching television, reading unedifying books or playing non-religious music on the piano. Until late in the twentieth century, Scottish society helpfully banned profane pursuits on Sundays, such as shopping or visiting public houses. The upside was that Sunday was the day when the saints opened their homes to each other, and rare was the Sunday when a nurse, a student or a visiting preacher did not join Jack and Nessie at their tea table.

The true communion of saints was the weekly Breaking of Bread, the format of which had changed little since Robert Haldane's time. The members put aside their worldly cares and united in meditation and praise. When the Spirit moved him, any baptised male member of the Hall was entitled to rise and read a passage from the Bible, on the basis of which he delivered a short homily, or prayed or 'gave out' a hymn from *The Believers Hymnbook*, whereupon the organist was immediately able to produce the music at the right pitch and pace for the assembly to join in.[1] It was only occasionally that his talent got the better of him and he confusingly embellished the backing track with virtuoso flourishes. Chief elder Donald McLean steered the order of play and generally kept the service within ninety minutes.[2] What he could not always steer was the Holy Spirit which, probably inadvertently, sometimes moved two men simultaneously. They would rise and declaim, focused entirely on their Lord or on their own inspired rhetoric, until they became aware of their wives tugging at the hem of their jackets. The more a man loved the sound of his own voice, the louder, longer and more self-regarding his mini sermon, but they were all heard out until Mr McLean cleared his throat and rose to say a prayer over the bread and wine.

Hymns for the morning meeting originally came from *Sankeys Sacred Songs and Solos*, then later the *Believers Hymn Book*, first published in 1889. It made sense that a favourite was the evangelical Charles Wesley's 'Jesu Lover of My Soul', but Nessie's favourite, 'Jesus, the very thought of thee', was written by a Cistercian abbot, Bernard of Clairvaux. Another much-loved hymn was 'Lord Jesus Christ, we seek Thy face' by Alexander Stewart. The words – 'Shut in with thee, far, far above the restless world that wars

---

1. In having an organ at the Breaking of Bread, Anniesland Hall was regarded by many other assemblies as heretical.
2. The Elders of the congregation carry the spiritual responsibilities of teaching, preaching, baptisms, marriages and funerals, often helped by visiting preachers – Anniesland Hall website.

below' – perfectly expressed both the siege mentality of the Brethren and their blissful adoration of the risen Lord, almighty and filling the room with His presence. Fired by the beauty of the words and the inspiring music, the assembly sang as one, all rivalry and sniping eclipsed by the soaring passion of requited love. It was a ritual, comforting and unifying, with none of the bluster of gospel services.

An argument against weekly communion is that it becomes routine, but this never seemed to be the case at Anniesland Hall. The service was never cancelled, not during the winter of power cuts where there was no heating in the building, not even during the bread strike of 1974, which cut off the supply of commercially made bread.[3] One Hall member was a professional baker but presumably he was unable to cross the picket line even in a private capacity, so Nessie, who had never made a non-fruit loaf in her life, had to bake the body of Christ. The communicants took this in their stride as, unlike the Catholics, they had never imagined the bread to be actual holy flesh, and also because the entire essence of the Hall was simplicity and spareness. To the Brethren, the images, statues and rituals the established churches employed to uplift the soul would have been a distraction from their intense personal relationship with their Saviour.

The relationship of the assembly members with the Trinity was complex. At children's meetings we were often enjoined: 'Don't think God is a nice old man with a long white beard'. They could have saved

---

3. But it was cancelled during the Covid-19 pandemic of 2020–22 (see postscript)

their breath. While the rites and occasional opacity of the Catholic and Anglican churches bestow a sense of divine mystery, the Plymouth Brethren, like fundamentalists of other faiths, created a God who was essentially in their own image – unpredictable, tender and forgiving, or vicious and intransigent.

Since men were able to create God, they could also decide what was sinful in the eyes of God, and at which points cruelty could be classed as just chastisement. God, although frequently addressed as a loving heavenly Father, appeared capricious, controlling, attention-seeking and violent, a kind of celestial domestic abuser.

Yet, while the Bible revealed God in His terrifying majesty, His servants were depicted as reassuringly human: God had to call Samuel's name three times before the prophet realised he was being summoned by the Almighty, and Peter, having announced that he would stand by Jesus, promptly denied Him thrice. What father could fail to be moved by the story of King David's rebellious son Absalom – who led a bloody but unsuccessful insurrection against his father and, while trying to escape, was caught by his long hair (grist to Brethren mills in the 1970s) in the branches of an oak tree and killed by the king's general while he hung there – or by David's searing lament when he heard of his son's death?[4] God's patience and forgiveness were immense but selective: when Uzzah put out his hand to stop the Ark of the Covenant

4. 2 Samuel 19:33. 'And the king was much moved, and went up to the chamber over the gate, and wept: and as he went, thus he said, O my son Absalom, my son, my son Absalom! would God I had died for thee, O Absalom, my son, my son!'

from falling off a wagon he was struck down in an instant;[5] Saul, though chosen of God, was flawed and allowed to fail; but David, beloved of God, exhibited a stunning catalogue of sins – lust, murder, adultery and betrayal – yet was forgiven time and again and granted the honour of being the ancestor of the Messiah.

Jesus, by contrast, was a source of wonder and admiration, a lover, a friend, an example to be followed. We pored over His every word and marvelled at His wisdom and moral strength. He was the risen Lord, who walked and talked with us along life's narrow way, a friend who never failed us, whose love would never die.

The third member of the Trinity was the Holy Spirit. Many assembly members worshipped a god who was neither a vengeful tyrant nor an authoritarian chastiser. They did not look for certainty in biblical verses whose meaning could be twisted one way or the other, but trusted that if they kept the risen Lord central to their being they would receive guidance and strength to act in a way that would honour Him. The heavenly Saviour would reveal himself to a questing heart and send his Holy Spirit to suffuse his servants, not only in the stillness of the night but also in the tumult of daily life. These humble worshippers looked at Jesus' mercy, humility and support for his brethren and for the needy, and followed the guidance of the Spirit. When their lives were joyful, they felt a

---

5. 2 Samuel 6:6, 7. 'And the anger of the Lord was kindled against Uzzah; and God smote him there for his error; and there he died by the ark of God.'

10. Fellowship

grateful, fulfilled gladness; when there were travails, they surrendered to the Lord's will and maintained a steadfast love and patient acceptance of undeserved pain.

This spiritual quietism was often more effectively activist than muscular evangelicalism. Led by the Spirit, his servants saw goodness and pain in others which, without fanfare, they sought to nurture or alleviate. They had courage too. A surgical nurse in her sixties spent two years aboard a Mercy Ship around the coast of Africa, providing healthcare and surgery for people with life-changing or disfiguring medical conditions. A sixty-year-old spinster smuggled bibles into the Soviet Union. On one occasion she was almost caught out at the airport, but quickly laid her coat over the offending books which passed unseen through security. She whispered, 'Thank you God', picked up her belongings and scuttled off.

The evening gospel meeting was entirely different from the breaking of bread. Given the imminence of the Last Judgment the saved had a duty to preach to the ungodly, and the elders ensured that a speaker and a singer were engaged to bear witness every Sunday evening. The hymns, from *Sankeys Sacred Songs and Solos*, were rousing. The pianist was able to let rip, or sometimes provide a sensitive accompaniment to a gifted soprano. But hymns and prayers were warm-ups for the main feature, the preacher, whose style would vary depending on which town or which assembly he was from.

Anniesland invited a range of preachers. There were professors from the university, often scientists or physics specialists who were able to reconcile science with the more problematic elements of the bible. There were thin, hard miners and shipbuilders who had been plucked from a life of drink and violence and shone with the joy of men whose little barks had found an anchor in a storm-tossed sea; or similar thin, hard miners and shipbuilders who channelled their former physical aggression into graphic descriptions of the horrors which awaited the unsaved; and there were trained evangelists who quoted the scriptures with facility and aptness, and seamlessly wove the latest news or trends into a persuasive, American-inflected narrative.

Most gripping were those who saw in current world events fulfilment of the scriptures, deducing that the Last Days were, again, upon us: in the 1960s 'the desert shall rejoice, and blossom as the rose' was held to be vindicated by the news that Israel had irrigated dry land and now produced and exported luscious fruit;[6] nation was indeed rising against nation as Israel occupied the Golan Heights and the Vietnam War escalated. Their eyes shining, this last group pulsated with joy and menace, for while gentle Jesus was calling the lambs unto Himself, He was also brandishing a gigantic cosmic bomb. Whatever the message or the messenger at these gospel meetings, few sinners were saved.

Those who were already saved found in Anniesland Hall a stimulating, supportive community. Many young men and women who had come to Glasgow from the Highlands and Islands, or even farther afield,

---

6. Isaiah 35:1

10. Fellowship

to study or become nurses, received a warm welcome. Young people met and married through the Hall, and the constant influx of new blood invigorated the community, which supported and sustained its own. When there was a bereavement, Hall members drew together, offering spiritual and practical support.

Jack, remembering the life-saving leadership qualities displayed by public school-educated naval officers, encouraged my brother Bill to sit the entrance exam for the Glasgow Academy, one of the top private schools in Glasgow. He had calculated that although the boy would not be accepted at the Academy, the experience of sitting the exam would make it easier when he applied for one of the many grant-assisted schools (like grammar schools) in the city. Not only did the boy pass the exam, but he was offered a bursary which covered his fees – but not his uniform, which was beyond family resources. The Hall stepped in, with individual members paying for components of the uniform – the blazer, the tie and so on. Loving generosity had unintended but foreseeable consequences – the boy knew he was from a lower rank than his schoolfellows, and although he worked hard at school and was accepted by St Andrews University, the responsibility weighed heavily on him. This was a downside of being part of a loving and mutually supportive community.

The At-Home (known as a Sworry in other assemblies – many years later I realised this was 'soiree') was another time for fellowship. On the last Saturday of January the post-Christmas gloom was brightened by a social event for all the members of the Hall. After initial greetings, the purvey (rhymes with scurvy) was served on long tables. Everyone received a white cardboard box from the City Bakeries containing a ham sandwich, a Tunnocks tea cake and an Eiffel tower – a two-inch high mini sponge cake covered in strawberry jam and dried coconut. Ice-cream and jelly came later in the evening. Then the fun began: quizzes, solos, perhaps a missionary slideshow, performances of Youth Praise songs by guitar-wielding teenagers, small plays performed by children, even a comedy pastiche of some of the members, who took it all in good part. It was light-hearted and uplifting, the older folk tolerating modern music and musical instruments and smiling indulgently at young actors, nodding appreciatively as each playlet ended on a moral note. There could be frowns if a child veered distantly towards blasphemy in a comedy routine, but there was only one major faux pas.

One Hall member had befriended her neighbour, a lovely young woman who regularly attended the Sunday evening services. She was a talented guitarist, and at one At-Home played and sang Ralph McTell's deeply humane 'Streets of London'. Performances were never applauded in any case, but the silence following her contribution was stony – it had been inappropriate to sing a 'pop' song in the Hall. She was later found sobbing in the toilets and was never seen again.

In summer, the members of the Hall were released from their stifling winter hats and coats. Summer was long sunny evenings when you could read without artificial light until 11.00 p.m. There was peace in the city, as the schools closed and the one o'clock horn at

10. Fellowship

the shipyards was silenced for the two weeks of the Glasgow Fair. The factories and yards shut down and the workers piled onto coaches bound for boarding houses in Troon, Blackpool and the Isle of Man, or returned to their families in the highlands and islands. For the Brethren, it was the time to head for Christian guesthouses in Largs or Larkhall, where they could relax with fellow believers from various assemblies.

Summer was the time when there was no Sunday School or Bible Class and the saints strolled down to the multi-assembly Sunday afternoon open-air service at the bandstand in Haldane's Victoria Park. It was the time for the Bible Class to hike over the hills then sing hymns by a barbecue on the banks of Loch Lomond, and the time for Sunday School trips when the children boarded hired corporation buses, tied streamers to the windows and sang choruses at the tops of their voices as they sped through the countryside to a playing field in some Lanarkshire village. There were games, races – and prizes.

Summer was also the time for the Assembly Sail. Every June, the Hall hired the *Countess of Breadalbane*, a 90-foot pleasure launch that accommodated 200 people, to take them to Millport on Great Cumbrae, an island in the Firth of Clyde. On the designated Saturday morning everyone rushed aboard a fleet of hired corporation buses parked outside the Hall. The young ones charged up to the top deck and set up streamers, stink bombs and thoroughly naughty versions of hymns and popular songs. A favourite substituted 'Blood of the Lamb' for 'Campbelltown Loch' – in other circumstances a capital offence, but the older folk downstairs could not, or chose not to, hear over the roar of the engine as the bus bowled along the Boulevard, past dreary Knightswood and Drumchapel, until the Clyde came into view.

The buses followed the course of the river, past Jackie Stewart's garage at Dumbuck,[7] and the platoon of geese guarding Ballantine's whisky warehouse, through Dumbarton and down to Craigendoran, where the *Countess* was waiting. The various generations headed for their favourite spots: mothers and older women in the saloon; men and young women on deck; children, when they had tired of running up and down the ladders, to the small saloon where they watched the pier moving away from the boat – no, the boat moving away from the pier – and settled down to whisper and giggle.

The women enjoyed cups of tea, refreshing for them but perhaps less so for the ferry operator Caledonia Steam Packet (later merged with MacBrayne's to form Calmac) which would have made its margins from selling alcohol. It is possible that Caledonian Steam Packet, like many venues where the brethren booked their wedding receptions, charged extra for no booze. On the other hand, given that many of Calmac ferries served the fiercely teetotal Hebrides, and did not run on Sundays until 2009, they may have had some sympathy with the Brethren.

The Sail was a time for fellowship. The young women paraded their full-skirted summer frocks, the

---

7. 'The Flying Scot' – a Formula One racing driver who won three world championships and did much to improve safety in racing cars and, by extension, family cars.

older women chatted, the men, barely recognisable without their Sunday suits, played with all the children. Millport, the only town on Cumbrae, is small. There were few cars then and Great Cumbrae was only 4.5 square miles, so when the ship docked there was no need to keep an eye on the older children, who were allowed to run free. The older folk headed for the tea shops, families hired bikes or played on the beach, and the teenagers made for the penny cakewalk at the funfair or clambered over the crocodile rock.[8] It was carefree and companionable.

By five o'clock the west coast evening was mellowing, fragrant and still. Everyone flocked back to the *Countess of Breadalbane*, watching eagerly from the deck for stragglers, and settled down to singing choruses in the saloon all the way home, little knowing that they were sailing in the wake of the ghosts of Oswald's ships bringing back tobacco from his slave plantations – the origins of the wealth and power of Anniesland Hall.

Summer was also the time for the Glasgow Summer Bible School. With its growing population of students and university professors, the Hall was in its heyday, brimming with thoughts and ideas. Blessed with superb premises, wealth from its financial assets and support from a vibrant congregation, the elders were eager to fulfil their duty of preaching the word and praising His name, albeit in this case only to the converted. Every September, Anniesland hosted a

---

8. This has nothing to do with the popular song by Elton John but is a crocodile-shaped rock which since before the First World War has been painted to resemble a friendly reptile.

month-long Glasgow Summer Bible School, attended on Monday and Friday evenings by hundreds of young people from Glasgow Assemblies for miles around. The noted Bible teacher George Harpur led the proceedings, introducing a specific theme each night so that attendees could split into groups for discussions under the guidance of mentors. Harpur was an Irish-born, former evangelist who had realised that Assembly Christians, long noted for their Bible knowledge, had lost this focus. Since many post-war young people were now university-educated, thanks to free tuition and generous, non-repayable, four-year personal grants (in Scotland), George Harpur saw that they were less in need of fulminations about the home-wrecking perils of the demon drink and more receptive to a sophisticated, analytical introduction to the wonders in the scriptures. Instead of a stick to beat 'wrong' thinking, the Bible should be a guide in daily Christian life and meditation. Nourished by the scriptures, young people could then go forth and witness.

In his urbane way, Harpur was adamant on the paramountcy of scripture, which 'lies fundamentally in the fact that it comes from God and must be vested with the authority of His sovereignty'. He acknowledged that 'private interpretation has, of course, its difficulties and risks' but maintained 'the individual's right and responsibility to understand the scripture for himself'.[9]

The Bible School was not the only occasion when individual assemblies joined with other Halls. Men visited other meetings to preach at their gospel services

---

9. Harpur, *Meet the Book*, p. 86.

and Brethren from across Glasgow joined forces in outreach campaigns, socials and young people's events. Twice a year, numerous assemblies came together for the Half-Yearlies, a week of fellowship and demonstrations of support for missionaries. The women contributed hand-embroidered table cloths, clothes and ornaments and home-made cakes to raise funds at the Missionary Sale of Work. Men and women attended bible study conferences and meetings, which culminated in the Missionary Rally in the Tent Hall, a large galleried auditorium built in 1876 for the Glasgow United Evangelistic Association, which before that had been meeting in a mission tent on Glasgow Green.

On Saturday evenings, traditionally a time when many fell prey to the 'demon drink', the Association had offered alternative entertainment of lantern slide shows illustrating the evils of alcohol and extolling the virtues of total abstinence. The Tent Hall, therefore, provided a relatively hallowed indoor space that accommodated 1,000 people, who flocked to the Missionary Rallies to hear uplifting tales from charismatic speakers. It was a window on the world and geopolitics as we heard of the cruelty of some regimes, like that of China, then in the throes of the Cultural Revolution. One missionary had been exiled from mainland China and, to his audience's great amusement, articulated Chinese tonal words. There were stories of women missionaries (not told publicly by the ladies themselves of course), recipients of miraculous help in adversity, such as the woman who had lain desperately ill for days, surrounded by rebels (it may have been in the Congo) and with only some cassava to eat. She was recounting this tale of woe to a doctor back in Britain who asked what her illness had been, and when he heard the nature of the complaint exclaimed 'but cassava is exactly what is prescribed for that!', leaving the lady praising the Lord for His mercy and begging forgiveness for doubting Him. The overriding themes of the Half-Yearlies were the power and blessings of the Lord and the constantly encroaching forces of evil, in ever-mutating guises – communism, cannibalism, Pentecostalism …

There was fellowship further afield. In the 1950s many young men and women entered missionary work, sometimes in countries they had been posted to in the war and had come to love. The Jackson mantelpiece was festooned with formal photos of smiling, neatly dressed missionary families. A major source of finance for missionaries, particularly those commended by Brethren Assemblies, was the magazine *Echoes of Service*. Its monthly newsletters depicted worlds far from grey post-war Glasgow, where intrepid young Scots kindled the aspirations of young Commonwealth citizens. Anniesland Hall had investment wealth and the disposable income of its members, and was generous in support of missionaries in the field and when they came home on furlough. Eric Kirton was one missionary sponsored by Anniesland Hall. He was sent to Malaya with the RAF in 1953 as part of the British response to the Emergency. The Plymouth Brethren had been established in Malaysia since 1859 and organised mission schools and church camps. At one of these camps, Kirton met and fell in love with a young Chinese-Burmese woman, Cheng Kim, and continued to correspond with her when he returned to Scotland. Luckily, in 1958 he heard 'the Call', returned to Malaya as a missionary and married Cheng Kim. Kirton was handsome, charismatic and devoted to his adopted home, in all its complexity, embodied in his lovely wife, although there was an element of risk in this – it was a time when Malay resentment was rising against the economically dominant ethnic Chinese.

But while missionaries like Eric Kirton were changing the world, the world itself was changing. When they returned on furlough many were discomfited by the contrast in morals between the Britain they had grown up in, the less worldly societies in their adopted towns and villages, and the 'permissive' Britain they had come back to. By the 1970s the value of the pound had plummeted and newly independent nations had become less than thrilled at the arrival of earnest young men lecturing them on how to live. Some countries granted entry only to missionaries with medical or teaching qualifications; some banned them altogether. As well as their triumphs, *Echoes* reported, in sorrow, the difficulties faced by the missionaries. Remarkably few met untimely ends and those were usually as a result of flying in rickety private planes to preach to tribes deep in the jungle. There were some martyrs. Five young American men were killed in Ecuador in 1955 and the resultant shockwaves reverberated in Anniesland Hall for decades. It was a reminder that giving one's life to Jesus could mean glorious martyrdom (resulting, in

Ecuador, in forgiveness by the victims' families and repentance and conversion of the perpetrators), rather than the puzzled indifference which usually met my proclamations of faith to the ungodly.

The post-war missionary effort, though not overtly supported by the British government, was an element of 'soft power'. Young people educated in missionary schools would often come to university in Britain with a commendation from their home assemblies. The Hall took them under its wing and contributed no doubt to favourable impressions of the Mother Country. Hospitable as ever, Nessie welcomed multiple young people from abroad, as well as missionaries and nurses from the western isles, to our home for tea, for chats, for Christmas dinner. The guests would often bring delicacies from their native lands as gifts. For us children, there were occasional disappointments, as when a French lady presented us with a pretty box of what appeared to be sweeties but turned out to be sugared almonds, severely deficient in the butter and sugar content required by Scottish tastebuds, while Cheng Kim's lychees resembled eyeballs too closely by far. On the whole these visits were a window on the world as we played with half-Scottish missionary children or puzzled to set the tales we heard from Bolivia or Malaysia against the context of grey post-war Britain.

'Pray for Belgium' was an exhortation on a card with a photo of the standard missionary family which stood on Jack and Nessie's mantlepiece. It is not clear why 1980s Belgium needed the intercession of the saints. Jack and Nessie may have known, they were relative globetrotters for the time. After a week staying with two children under ten in a bed and breakfast in Troon when it rained all day every day – in those days guests were not allowed to return between breakfast and bedtime – they decided to go abroad, or rather Southport, for better weather. This was a first in Anniesland Hall. Apart from missionaries and businessmen, no one ventured south of the border. The Jacksons became bolder. While Jack, after six years at sea, had sworn he would never go abroad again, Nessie longed to see the art and architecture of Europe, so the family sailed for Belgium in 1968. It was certainly a benighted country, Jack delighting in identifying 'the old pineapple' (chapel) prominent in each village, with the Romanism leavened by plucky little outposts of Plymouth Brethren. The Brethren worldwide published a handbook with the contact details of every assembly on the planet, so we dressed in our Sunday clothes and hats and headed from Belgium to the closest, in Lille. As always, the chief elder welcomed us to their fellowship and we settled down to hymns in the French language, but with familiar tunes.

Holidays in England similarly involved dressing in Sunday best and receiving a welcome from whichever assembly was nearest to the holiday location. It was an opportunity for making contacts and experiencing the generosity and love of strangers – in other words, fellowship.

> Be ye not unequally yoked together with unbelievers: for what fellowship hath

righteousness with unrighteousness? And what communion hath light with darkness? Wherefore come out from among them, and be ye separate, saith the Lord, and touch not the unclean thing; and I will receive you.
2 Corinthians 6:14,17.

One holiday in England included a visit to John Baker, a Brethren acquaintance who owned a farm and a beautiful house in Chelmsford, Essex. Baker had served with Jack in Malta and the wartime bonds were never sundered. We were invited to lunch but I, aged nine and overawed by the grand surroundings, misbehaved and was removed from the dining room by my mother. We went into the adjoining room where we saw the Bakers' daughter, a nurse, eating her meal alone. When I asked why, Nessie explained that the young woman had refused to be baptised – the Bakers were Close Brethren and could not sit down to eat with her. As a Plymouth Brethren website explains, 'those in fellowship must ultimately exercise their own judgment in the practice of separation from those (family, friends, colleagues) who choose to leave the Brethren community'. Yet Jesus sat down to eat with publicans and sinners, and Miss Baker was a nurse, not a prostitute. It was a puzzle.

11. Service

Many members of Anniesland Hall chose caring professions, or used their professional positions to make a positive difference in the city and beyond. Several served in the mission field as teachers and nurses, and support for missionaries was still strong. But Jack longed to do more.

When they graduated from Jordanhill College, Jack and Nessie soon found work in Glasgow schools. Jack taught at Church Street School in Partick for twenty years, then as a deputy headmaster at Barrowfield in Bridgeton, in Glasgow's east end. The catchment area for Church Street, partly on Byres Road in the university area, covered children of shipyard workers and white-collar workers. Barrowfield was and remains rough. In 2020 it was still in the top five per cent most deprived areas in Scotland. In such schools teachers could have immense influence for good, in health and well-being as well as education. The legendary football manager Sir Alex Ferguson recalled his teacher at Broomloan Primary in Govan, Elizabeth Thompson (a friend and colleague of Jack's) going round the houses of all her pupils who had not turned up and telling the parents: 'If your kid isn't in school tomorrow, I'll be back at your door. If you get your kid into school, I'll make something of them. That's all you need to do – get them there. I'll do the rest."[1] Jack shared this determination to bring out the best. He was closely involved with the community, at one point delivering a baby and on another day being assaulted by a parent with a cornflakes packet. He was not soft, and certainly not enlightened – long after he retired 'Quick-on-the-draw Jackson' would often be greeted by former pupils who remembered the Lochgelly tawse he wore under the shoulder of his jacket so it could be whipped instantly into service.[2] But his constant focus was to make good productive citizens of the children in his care. He led successful Saturday morning football teams, organised school trips to museums and even the ballet, advocated for children in court, and gave after-school tuition to struggling pupils, often in his own home. One such pupil was the child of publicans who showed their appreciation by bringing him a huge box of assorted bottles of booze – Jack returned it with thanks.

Since his days in the navy Jack had always honoured authority. He was delighted when his friend David McNee, a committed Christian and Chief Constable of the City of Glasgow Police, became head of the Metropolitan Police. He enjoyed working with police officers to manage his pupils' skirmishes with the law. Through these acquaintances he became involved in the Glasgow police's road and home safety quiz, which was open to all the primary schools in Glasgow. Contestants came from all backgrounds,

---

1. *Glasgow Herald*, 7 November 1998
2. A leather strap with one end split into narrow strips.

but the winners tended to be children from middle-class or private schools. Jack coached teams from Church Street School and rejoiced when they carried off the trophy on several occasions. The children of Barrowfield had none of the advantages that even the Church Street pupils enjoyed, but Jack saw the competition as an opportunity for these children to learn some rudiments of safe behaviour, to practise speaking in front of an audience and, maybe, enjoy the satisfaction of making it past the first round. In the event, his pupils responded so well to his coaching that they reached the final, up against a much more privileged school.

At the final, on a mellow June evening, they maintained their composure, answered the questions clearly and confidently and won the city-wide competition to great acclaim from Jack, the Barrowfield head teacher, the audience and the police. After the tension of the quiz there was an exciting display from police dogs who fetched, leapt obstacles of increasing heights and brought a heavily gloved policeman to the ground (perhaps less of a novel sight to the Barrowfield children than to my brother and me).

It was still light after the event so Jack drove us to Loch Lomond where we tried to persuade the family dog to repeat the feats we had witnessed that evening and Jack absorbed his small yet giant achievement. His own son and daughter, he knew, would go on to good universities and a fulfilling career, but that day poor, malnourished and slightly malodorous children had also seized their chance to shine, to be congratulated heartily by men they would normally hate and fear, to receive a medal and a prize and believe, even for one night, that they were masters of their fate.

Perhaps this achievement helped Jack win the prize he had longed for, to be deputy headmaster at the white-collar Broomhill Primary School where Elizabeth Thompson taught (having moved on from Govan). He stayed at Broomhill until he retired, but found that all he had to do there was teach and he missed the drama and pastoral responsibilities at Bridgeton.

Still Jack burned to serve. To his lasting regret (and our relief) Jack never received the Call to serve the Lord in the mission field. However, service comes in many forms and Jack found opportunities for mission work in his own country. He and many of the men in Anniesland Hall often preached at other assemblies in the central belt of Scotland, and at the Glasgow Seamen's Mission, but Jack's most dedicated service was in Drumchapel.

The common parts in Anniesland Mansions brought common duties, one of which was that each tenant's wife took her turn to wash the stairs, a practice which was dealt an inadvertent blow after the Second World War by the Glasgow City Fathers. Recalling the failure of successive national governments to make good on Lloyd George's promise to provide 'homes fit for heroes' returning from the First World War, the Labour City Council were determined not to repeat this mistake and built vast new housing schemes in the fresh air of the surrounding countryside. As Glasgow's housing convenor, Councillor James Duncan, put it in 1951, 'Glasgow folk have been through hell. We are going to build so many houses that this second city will be a housing paradise on earth.'³

The housing schemes were poorly planned and shoddily built. As people were decanted from the city centre, community ties were broken, and easy access to the countryside meant little to urban folk for whom the estates were, as the comedian Billy Connolly put it, 'deserts wi' windaes'.

The Drumchapel estate, built in the 1950s, was to house 34,000 people, but the planners neglected to build schools, which for years were located in commandeered blocks of flats, and omitted to provide shops and pubs. To add to the isolation of Drumchapel, it was not served by the green and orange Corporation buses, but by the privately-owned Alexander's 'Blue buses' which passengers could board within Glasgow, but not leave until beyond the city boundary. Anniesland Cross was on major tram and bus routes, and it was here that the men of Drumchapel, particularly on a Friday evening after work, would change from Corporation to Blue buses after a drinking session in town.

Conveniently, 1605 Great Western Road was just by the bus stops, convenient also for vomiting, urinating, defecating or lying in a drunken stupor in the close. We would often have to step over men lying semi-conscious on the stairs, terrified that they might in fact be dead, and whichever lady was on the cleaning rota that week would have to wash up the mess. As all the tenants of 1597 and 1605 had been carefully vetted, these ladies had never touched a drop

---

3. *Glasgow Herald* 7 November 1998

of alcohol in their lives and it is unsurprising they were unable to see any gradation between total abstinence and the swaying, stinking, vomiting by-products of the Demon Drink.

Of the 34,000 souls in Drumchapel, many had been torn from their original communities in the city slums and now had no access to a local church. Anniesland Hall had a corrugated iron hut where the small assembly gathered to break bread on Sunday mornings and carry out 'outreach' in the form of a Sunday school with 200 pupils, a boys' club, a girls' club and a Sunday night cafe. Jack, his old wartime friend George Stewart, Duncan Stephen and Alec Birss, the owner of a department store in Partick, devoted much time and energy to Drumchapel. In a poor, deprived area where children had never seen the sea and who, although they could have run directly from their front doors onto fields and hills, rarely ventured there, Drumchapel Hall provided activities in the fresh air, including football matches and Sunday School trips to the country. Jack did not attend Drumchapel's evening meeting or the Friday night boys' club, which were led by Duncan, as he was often on the road preaching to other assemblies, but every other Sunday, after he had opened up Anniesland Hall and set the heating, he faithfully journeyed out to Drumchapel while Nessie took care of my brother and me. In those days, when divorce was rare, it transpired that a newish member of Anniesland had long assumed that Nessie was a widow.

Jack served the people of Temple, a district adjacent to Anniesland, for many years, particularly in the CYC (Christian Youth Centre) for young teenagers every Friday evening in winter. In keeping with the Brethren desire for separation from the world, the CYC intentionally provided the Hall children with an alternative to Scouts, Brownies or the Boys Brigade, but it was also a means of reaching out to young people from within that world. There were prayers, choruses and a short sermon, but most of the time was spent on arts and crafts in one of the larger side halls. The children learnt to express themselves and produced objects which were put on sale at the end of the year, while obtaining professional skills – Jack's best man Gary Walker brought in his printing press and the boys printed visiting cards and notices.

Partly regenerated since, Temple at the time was a relatively rough working class area.[4] The children were skinny, pale and unkempt, sometimes gently shepherding siblings with heart-rending disabilities, but they had the confidence to cross Great Western Road – something of a Rubicon to me – to attend the CYC, working together companionably with the Hall children on the handicrafts and joining cheerfully in the singing.

In summer the CYC met for rounders in Dawsholm Park on the north side of the canal. Hall and Temple children played happily together, up to a point, but no lasting friendships were formed. The Hall children had become so insulated from the wider

---

4. Stones were thrown at me when, having got on the wrong bus, I walked through Temple in my school uniform. This tribalism was not unique – we could use the swing park next to a middle-class block down Crow Road only by prior invitation, although the children there relied on glowers rather than missiles to defend their territory.

world that we were unable to relate to the pleasures and pains of the children from Temple.

Much more successful was another of Jack's inspirations – a candlelit carol service on the Sunday evening before Christmas. Up to this point Christmas Sunday had been a dispiriting affair. Of course there had always been a Sunday School Christmas party (on a Saturday) when the seating was cleared away and little boys in smart shirts and little girls in party dresses tumbled around in games and quizzes then sat quiet as mice when the lights were turned down and Santa's bell tinkled ever closer till he burst into the room, jovial and bearing a huge sack. There were carols at Sunday School and occasionally in the evening service, but the meeting on Christmas Sunday morning, even if it was Christmas Day, studiously avoided any mention of jollity or even joy.

As late as 1996, by which time there was a specific Christmas Day morning service, sin was mentioned six times in the sermon, presents were only mentioned in order to segue into God's great gift to us – a picture of Christ crucified. A four-year-old, on being asked what was special about the day, replied that it was Jesus' birthday. It was only when prompted by the preacher that the child remembered it was his birthday too.

Jack saw the rising popularity of Christmas services in the 1970s, originating in England, and decided that the devil should not have all the best tunes nor, in the case of the Anglican church, the best services, which included candles. He had to fight hard with his fellow elders on this – candles equalled Papism, unless they were on a birthday cake or resorted to in a power cut – but he prevailed. Nessie designed posters advertising the event, the heating was turned on in the Big Hall days in advance, assembly members were detailed to sit with candles and matches in designated spots in the tiered seating, and local people crowded in. The Big Hall was almost full, cosy and humming with anticipation. Jack stood on the platform by a glittering Christmas tree and welcomed all comers. Lightening the atmosphere with a few jokes as he always did, he led the assembled company in spirited renditions of well-loved carols, waving his arms and rousing them to sing their hearts out. The Bible Class choir impressed, the Sunday School choir delighted, and, after a notably hell-free sermon, the candles were lit, the lights went down and the words of the best-loved carols were projected onto the apse behind Jack. All eyes were raised, all hearts were uplifted as the dainty flickering of the candles cast mysterious shadows on the vaulted roof and the slender pillars, and the people sang sweet and low. No one was saved, but in their souls everyone embraced the comfort and joy of the Christmas story.

Blood of the Lamb

6. Jack and his pupils

12. Going Into All the World to Preach the Gospel

On Sunday evenings our father would read to us from the Jungle Doctor stories written by a missionary, Paul White. In one tale, a monkey discovered that sacks of nuts had been stored in a mud hut. The monkey managed to squeeze his paw through a gap in the wall and grab a handful of nuts. Alas, the farmer saw him. A chill entered our hearts when we looked at an illustration of the monkey looking up in terror as a huge cudgel was brought down on his head. If he had relinquished the nuts the monkey could have been saved, but he clung on to his theft, his sin.

The 1950s and 1960s were days of renewed enthusiasm. America was still the land of opportunity, brimming with confidence – and marketing. The American evangelist Billy Graham was a major international figure, organising gospel crusades and training young men in the art of modern communications. Dr Graham held a crusade in Glasgow in 1955, attended by thousands. Glasgow Corporation authorised all third-year pupils to take the afternoon off and go to the rallies.[1] In the 1960s, Graham was not available in person so the assemblies hired a cinema in the centre of the city to show a film of one of his rallies. The film played to full houses throughout. Jack and Nessie had been nominated to go down and counsel people who wanted be saved. At the closing hymn, the emotive 'Just as I am', all who wanted to give their hearts to Jesus were told to go down to the front. Nessie instructed Bill to hold my hand and announced they were going to the front, much to my consternation – I thought Jack and Nessie were going down to be saved and quailed at the thought of how much more religious the household could become. So many counsellors flocked to the front that it is difficult to estimate how many new converts there were, but the giant American on the screen, reinforced by the massed ranks of his choirs, had presented the right mix of threat and persuasion to reap hundreds of souls. It was an American event such as few had experienced before, and few were equipped to fully resist.

Although televangelism never took off in Britain, professional outreach was in vogue. Numbers of young men abandoned promising careers and studied at Billy Graham training institutes in America. They returned fired with zeal and replete with Americanisms, impatiently waiting for invitations to

---

1. Third year in secondary school, that is, pupils in the year before taking GCSEs.

12. Going Into All the World to Preach the Gospel

preach the gospel. The invitations came; for one-night events, week-long evening bible schools, and for two-week crusades under the auspices of SCEM (Scottish Counties Evangelistic Movement). At the invitation of local assemblies in smaller towns across Scotland, SCEM would arrange for a preacher and teams of young people to descend for two weeks and carry out a gospel campaign. The young folk slept on camp beds in local schools, supervised by 'house parents'. Jack and Nessie, as teachers on their school summer holidays, were ideal candidates and volunteered for three successive years, 1970–72, in Montrose, Lockerbie and Stirling. Jack had the right blend of fun and discipline, while Nessie had a gentle touch and twenty years' experience as both a teacher and head of her own private school. The young people were sent round the town with personal invitations to all the residents, and organised coffee mornings and clubs with games and quizzes for children. The evangelist preached the gospel to the masses in the evenings and led bible studies for the Christian young folk during the day. It was an uplifting experience, learning and praying together, pulling together in the service of the Lord, and often meeting life partners.

One of the young women on the team at Montrose was a beautiful but haughty schoolteacher who ended up in the tabloids for having sex with a pupil. Even more salacious that year was the nearby Aberdeen Incident, when Jim Taylor, the American leader of the Exclusive Brethren who had a notorious drink problem, was found in bed with a married woman who was not his wife. Many were the preachers who fell at this hurdle, despite their loud condemnations of the slightest deviation from the Way. Arthur Blessitt, a Southern Baptist from Mississippi, was an energetic and imaginative showman, acquainted with heads of state and known for carrying a huge cross through every country in the world. He had courage, visiting war-torn areas, and charisma. Unlike the usual Billy Graham lookalikes, the long-haired Arthur Blessitt wore jeans and a leather waistcoat, whipped up wild enthusiasm and gave everyone orange 'Smile – Jesus loves you' stickers. Young people flocked to his rallies in the Tent Hall in 1972 and cheered, waved their arms and embraced the joy of Jesus. It was suddenly exciting to be a Christian. Blessitt's preaching inspired young people to channel their enthusiasm into bringing the unsaved to God, the same God who, Blessitt maintained, told him to divorce his first wife and the mother of his six children, and marry a model thirty years his junior.

Perhaps a successful evangelist has to be a risk-taker; perhaps their self-proclaimed position as God's messenger leads them believe they too can walk on water; perhaps their own eloquence persuades them of the innocence of their intentions; perhaps hubris is what empowers them to harangue sinners in the first place. Whatever the case, Jack took us to hear several famous preachers and, during my research for this book, I found that many had succumbed in spectacular fashion to the lusts of the flesh.

The lusts of the flesh were an ever-present danger. Sorrowful retribution was swift. On two occasions, in my memory, assembly members were 'read out',

12. Going Into All the World to Preach the Gospel

or banned from the breaking of bread. At the end of the morning meeting Donald MacLean requested all who had not been baptised to leave the room. The atmosphere was thick with tension and suppressed excitement. Mr MacLean then announced that one of our number, a self-important businessman whose contributions to the morning meeting invariably included boasting about his business trips to America, had been seen coming down the stairs of the North British hotel in Edinburgh with 'a woman who was not his wife'. The frisson was heightened by the presence of his wife and two teenage children sitting rigid in their Sunday coats and hats. The man was then duly read out. Disappointingly, if perhaps unconvincingly, just before we filed out we were informed that 'no immoral act took place', and he was later read back in again.

On the other occasion, an engaged couple were read out for premarital sex, but they too were read straight back in again and permitted to marry in the Hall.

My husband and I did not get off as lightly and were not allowed to marry in the Hall because we had been living together. Worse, my Anglican fiancé argued, using a bible concordance as evidence,[2] that fornication is mentioned far fewer times in the bible than anger, unwittingly compounding his sin with a jaw-dropping exemplar of the sin of pride. We were married instead by a dear friend in St Paul's, a

---

2. A concordance is an alphabetical list of the important words present in a biblical text, usually with citations of the passages in which they are found.

beautiful, eighteenth-century, Anglo-Catholic church in Deptford, followed by a reception in the seedy Deptford Arms. My parents agreed to pay for the reception but not for any alcohol. When they sent out the invitations the venue had been mysteriously transmogrified into 'the Deptford Arms Hotel'.

Fiascos come easily to the zealous. One particularly keen young member of the Hall was out canvassing and became engaged in conversation with a thin, long-haired fellow who accepted his invitation to come to the evening meeting. The stranger sat meekly throughout the service and shared my bible. At the young folks' meeting after the service the man gave his testimony, which included the women he had had sex with under African skies and the drugs he had enjoyed – all presumably now jettisoned for the Lord. It was all an act. Three days later he was seen in town wearing blue eyeshadow. It turned out that he was David Hayman, a successful and versatile actor in films, television and documentaries, and also an individual of integrity who founded the charity Spirit Aid.[3] His motivation for the stunt at Anniesland is unknown.

By the 1970s, Hall members were becoming uncomfortably aware that Anniesland Hall was increasingly an affluent, mutually reinforcing club, with little effect on the community beyond its doors. Instead of shining Jesus' light throughout the world, the Brethren were basking in its cosy glow. The

---

3. A Scottish humanitarian relief organisation dedicated to alleviating the suffering of children and young people whose lives have been affected by poverty, neglect, abuse, lack of opportunity, humanitarian crisis or even blighted by war.' From Spirit Aid's website.

unsaved were becoming less identifiable as the state provided better education, housing and healthcare and the heavy industries entered their final decline. Brave little open-airs and the distribution of tracts to passers-by yielded little but discarded sheets of paper fluttering in the wind. The Hall's main efforts at outreach were evening open-air meetings ignored by the television-watching unsaved, and homilies delivered in the city centre, which sparked the interest of sundry drunks but no one else.

David Hayman had clearly been a damp squib, but the elders were undeterred, conscious that they were blessed with money, willing participants and connections, but no converts. It was time to go into all the world and preach the gospel – and the World could not have had a more physical manifestation than the Odeon cinema across the road. The elders set a budget of over £1,000 for a week's Gospel Campaign. Jack planned the events with method and imagination, delegating, allocating and motivating: Nessie painted advertising posters; Gary Walker printed leaflets which were delivered by carefully co-ordinated teams; adverts were placed in the Glasgow Herald; members of the other assemblies in Glasgow were urged to attend – and did, by the score; selected saints from all the assemblies were deployed as counsellors, located strategically so they could identify searching souls and bring them to the Lord. The Odeon was ideal for intensity and creeping menace. Soloists sang, the audience belted out gospel tunes, preachers threatened and entreated, and the audience softly crooned:

> Just as I am, without one plea
> But that Thy blood was shed for me
> And that Thou bid'st me come to thee
> O Lamb of God, I come, I come.

At least three were saved, all from Temple: John, a dapper ex-offender and current dustman; Joe, obese and somewhat miasmal, who clearly had glandular problems; and Evelyn, bristling with the secret vulnerability of the hard as nails.

The exaltation of saving souls was not underpinned by an awareness that the mortals inhabited by these souls needed long-term nurturing and guiding. This was an issue increasingly identified by Brethren thinkers such as John Allan, who cautioned that 'New Testament methods of evangelism which do not lead into a New Testament commitment to teach, guide and shepherd the new Christian will never result in very much'.[4] It was not for nothing that Jesus was known as the Good Shepherd, but the rub was that, like the Good Shepherd, the members at Anniesland were an entirely different species from the lost sheep.

The saints did their best. The three converts were invited frequently to tea, and joined the young folks at the Sunday evening gatherings in members' houses, but those houses were dauntingly prosperous, and the confidence, education and aspirations of the Hall young folk estranged them even more from their target group of publicans and sinners.[5] Comfort and security had blunted their understanding of converts'

---

4. Allan, 'The Local Church and Evangelism', pp. 16–20.
5. Matthew 9:10. 'As Jesus sat at meat in the house, behold, many publicans and sinners came and sat down with him and his disciples.'

12. Going Into All the World to Preach the Gospel

existing social and family groups, their circumstances and mindsets, and the type of support they would need to flourish in the competitive arena of the Hall.

There are few entirely stable individuals who respond to the Call at gospel outreach services, and these three, although genuinely searching for meaning in their lives, were no exception. Joe was surly and socially inadequate, Evelyn lacked all the advantages which were taken for granted by the young people of the Hall. John was handsome, often seen hanging off the back of his bin wagon giving a cheery wave to any young girls on the pavement, and was mystified as to why he should suddenly reject his unsaved friends and his pub.

For the Hall insisted that repentant sinners forsake all else to follow Him – and to adopt the lifestyle of its members, who were increasingly middle-class professionals, and whose children were confident and sophisticated. The ex-miners, shipbuilders and former alcoholics delivering impassioned testimonies at the gospel service were often the object of ill-concealed mirth among the teenagers and university students in the audience. The success of members in bringing up their children to fear the Lord meant that these same children had no concept that the unsaved could also lead decent, honourable lives.

As a small child, when I saw the Queen on television I worried about the embarrassment she would suffer, arriving at heaven's gate only to be told that it was all very well being head of the Church of England, but she had not been saved. As with all sects and some political parties, the members of Anniesland

Hall had become unable to value the views of people of other persuasions, or to compromise on their demands, and few understood the inner conflicts which beset Evelyn.

Evelyn was not prepossessing. She was short and dumpy, with a large head and small eyes in a face with the greyish, rough-textured skin common to many children and young people from the Glasgow slums, the result of poor nutrition and exposure to pollutants from babyhood. Stumping around in disproportionately high heels, tight skirts and tighter blouses, she exuded wary menace, but she had courage. She and her mother lived on benefits in a small flat in Temple, where they lacked the support of an extended family and relied on their obstinacy and their wits. She and her companions had come to the Odeon out of curiosity, for a laugh, but in the vast darkness of the cinema, Evelyn, a fan of Tamla Motown, was transfixed by a combination of the fervour and joy of the audience and the emotional power of the music. The evangelist proclaimed the love and power of God to a young woman yearning for love and a chance to belong in a world beyond her limited horizons, and she moved with the others down to the front where they stood with bowed heads as the preacher praised the Lord and prayed over them.

The new converts were greeted by counsellors. Clarice Stephen, a teacher whose husband Duncan had spent six years in a German POW camp (escaping three times), volunteered to shepherd Evelyn on the path of righteousness. For Evelyn this was a door opening into a world of warmth and encouragement as Clarice had the devotion of a woman who had a teacher's mission to support and inspire, and the kindness of a strong but gentle soul. Evelyn was a frequent guest at the Stephens' home in Bearsden, a comfortable town on the edge of Glasgow,[6] where Clarice attempted to guide the young woman on her spiritual path while teaching her basic domestic and social skills – for Evelyn had never smelt the aroma of home baking permeating a cosy well-ordered home, or witnessed the intricacies of bone china, linen and decorated teaspoons, which were essential elements of a Scottish afternoon tea. The young people in the Hall tried to make Evelyn, Joe and John welcome, but it was always on their terms – no alcohol or cigarettes of course, and the biggest excitement was drinking coffee and singing hymns after the Sunday night service. The intellectual young men – and there were several who obtained firsts at the best universities and went on to successful careers in the professions – displayed their wit with in-jokes and biblical word play, rather than contemplating the mysteries of the gospel, which having been part of their experience from the cradle, were no longer mysteries. They did not pause to consider how to bridge the gap – 100 yards or a million miles – between Temple and Anniesland Hall.

Clarice saw this, and spoke gently of her Lord to Evelyn, encouraging her to seek more deeply and put her trust in the Lord's love for her. She saw that if Evelyn did not find a way to make herself the equal of her fellow Christians, she would feel she did

---

6. Bearsden was ranked the seventh-wealthiest area in Britain in a 2005 survey and has the least social housing of any town in Scotland.

not belong, and would fall by the wayside. Clarice encouraged Evelyn to apply for a course at the local further education college, but this young woman, who had fought her way through life to that point, resisted a reversion to the powerlessness of being a pupil. Her mentor then obtained a place for Evelyn as a school dinner lady – a regular job, with potential. Evelyn struggled at work. Aunt Clarice managed to win several second chances for her, despite persistent late-coming, but when Evelyn was spotted in the school kitchens crawling with head lice, Clarice could do nothing to rescue her. As her mentor lamented, Evelyn could be described as the perpetrator of the late-coming, but was surely the victim in the headlice affair.

Another Hall member took an interest in Evelyn – I did. Mindful of paternal reminders that my life was undeservedly easy and privileged, and straining to escape the Anniesland straitjacket, I had become fascinated by the World. My schoolfriends smoked, drank, listened to Leonard Cohen and The Doors and took a place at university for granted. In those heady days of the UCS work-in (see Chapter 13) and the three-day week, they supported the miners and the shipbuilders. They expressed their own opinions on issues where Jack had insisted his children defer to their elders, using 'bourgeois' as the ultimate insult for anything to the right of Marxism. To me, Evelyn provided an opportunity to share my material good fortune with someone less fortunate, a chance to sample 'real' (i.e. working class) people, and an entrée to Temple – for I too wanted to belong. I invited Evelyn often to my home, then to a party at my schoolfriend's house, where smoking and (underage) drinking was the norm. Alas, at the party the genuine working-class article was greeted with horror and, since the choice was Evelyn or my schoolfriends, Evelyn was thrown under the bus.

But Evelyn was a fighter. She stuck with the Hall for many years, was a key member of the Anniesland Singers, a gospel choir, and remained a committed Christian all her too-short life. But in the Hall, Evelyn became increasingly aware of her failure to make the grade. The Tamla fan was thrilled to go through to Edinburgh with the young folk to see Andraé Crouch and the Disciples, an African-American gospel choir led by Crouch, a singer, songwriter and associate of Paul Simon, Michael Jackson and Stevie Wonder. While Evelyn was delighted with the performance, the Hall young folk sniggered at the choir's gowns and synchronised gestures.

Evelyn, who had hoped for a safe haven in Jesus, was being cast again onto the stormy seas of isolation and failure. Her attempts to cast off the sins of smoking, drinking and sex led to isolation in her own community and the unexpected problem that, without her cigarette lighter, she could no longer find the housekey her mother left under a stone outside the front door. The Lord no longer seemed to hear her prayers and the very people who had enticed her into their midst constantly evolved their definition of sin or unworthiness to include most of Evelyn's pleasures. When she conquered smoking, she fell short of the glory of God in new, endless mutations, and was beginning to be aware of her bi-sexual nature. Evelyn eventually moved further along Great Western Road to St Mary's, the first cathedral in Britain to welcome same-sex marriage in church. When she died at the age of fifty-three, widely praised for her selfless work as a carer, she was buried by a church which did not see her way of loving as a sin.

But what is sin? According to the Oxford English Dictionary, sin is 'transgression of divine law; violation of a religious or moral principle'. For adherents of some faiths and churches, divine law is defined by a recognised authority; for many Protestant denominations, where individuals have a direct relationship with God, sin is defined to these individuals by God, and can be described as 'any action that harms the relationship we have with God and/or another person'.[7]

According to the Bible, sin is inherent in every human – 'for we are born in sin and shapen in iniquity'. As a consequence, sin is self – self-will, self-indulgence, selfishness, self-love or pride. Since divine law is perfect, only our self-will causes us to transgress; if morals are immutable, violating them is the action of the iniquitous self. Yet morals seem to be infinitely mutable. Until recently the practice of homosexuality was universally regarded as a sin, but in many countries and denominations it is now seen as another manifestation of love. In 1960 many Hall members believed it was a sin to watch television; in 1966 it was a sin to watch television on Sundays; when Apollo 11 landed on the moon on Sunday 20 July 1969, watching it live was not a sin, but an

---

7. www.compellingtruth.org

opportunity to marvel at God's wonders; by 1990 the *Antiques Road Show* was a pleasant way to relax on a Sunday evening after a busy schedule of services.[8] What was a sin in one circumstance was an innocent pleasure in another. Some members of Anniesland Hall were tending to savour God's gifts, rather than second-guessing what His views on alcohol would be in 1980 as opposed to 30 CE when He provided the finest wine for a wedding in Cana. When I asked my mother why Jesus could drink wine, which we regarded as a sin, I was told that in those days it wasn't safe to drink the water; others pointed out that there is no evidence that Jesus had actually drunk any. Yet if alcohol could be seen in a historical context, somehow the issue of head coverings for women could not.

The key to identifying sin is the concept of intent, whether television watching or chocolate eating, or wilful and prideful distancing from God. This was the minefield that Evelyn, John Ross and, before them, the young woman singing Ralph McTell at the At-Home, were tiptoeing through. What the Hall members could instinctively identify as sin, or at least separation from God, was indecipherable to young people from communities with other norms and habits. A side effect of the absence of Church dogma was arbitrariness, leaving the naïve and unwary struggling to discern the thin line between right and downright wrong. They stumbled and fell.

---

8. A long-running BBC television programme in which experts travel to various British locations and give valuations of antiques brought in by local people.

13. The Winds of Change

On 4 May 1970 twenty-eight National Guard soldiers fired approximately sixty-seven rounds of ammunition at students holding a peaceful anti-Vietnam war protest on the campus of Kent State University, Ohio. Nine students were wounded and four died, among them nineteen-year-old Allison Krause. Watching Krause's weeping father being interviewed on television, Jack stiffened: 'Yes, the man's crying, he's lost his daughter. But she broke the law.' How had it come to this?

The pre-war certainties were crumbling. Although shipbuilding on the Clyde was not finally humbled until the 1970s, it had always been a precarious business, subject to cyclical downturns and trade distortions, and constantly having to evolve in the wake of developments in technology from sail to steam then turbines, and from wood to iron to steel. Since Clyde shipbuilders specialised in naval vessels, steamers and liners, they were subject to fluctuations in demand due to wars, economics and fashion. In the boom years of 1913–14 when Britain was engaged in a naval race with Germany, eighteen per cent of the

13. The Winds of Change

world's new ships were Clyde-built, and after the First World War capacity was expanded in anticipation of a post-war boom, which was stopped in its tracks by the Depression. Hopes were again raised in the 1930s with the construction of the Cunard liners the *Queen Mary* and the *Queen Elizabeth*, but war intervened and when the *Queen Elizabeth* entered service in February 1940 it was as a troopship, with her Cunard livery of black hull and red funnel painted over in battleship grey.

When the war was over the world had changed again. Transatlantic liner crossings became less popular with the advent of the Jet Age; Japan and South Korea overtook the Clyde in terms of cost and technology. Yards began to close, followed by their suppliers, steelworks and engineering works. The Clyde had indeed 'made Glasgow', yet in some respects shipbuilding also proved to be the city's undoing. Central governments have long subsidised shipbuilding, believing it to be essential to a nation's trade and security as it guarantees a supply of merchant vessels and warships, and supports ancillary steel, coal and iron industries, as well as subcontracted trades. However, subsidies encourage over-capacity and an unwillingness to diversify, and the Clydeside unions were strong and initially opposed to change.

In 1968, in an effort to achieve economies of scale and to satisfy increasing demand for bigger merchant ships, five upper Clyde yards were amalgamated into Upper Clyde Shipbuilders (UCS). By June 1971 the consortium was still making losses, so the government withdrew its subsidies and UCS went into receivership. Glasgow sank into deep gloom. We children feared, without comprehending, spectres like 'the Receiver' and 'arbitration'. In the streets, working-age men, normally invisible in the daytime, shopped, grim-faced, with their anxious wives. Like a mediaeval army, shipyard workers marched silently through Glasgow bearing their glorious union banners aloft, but no girls cast roses at their feet, no trumpets blew; these were battalions marching towards defeat. There was a principled, heroic 'work-in' at the yards when, as a riposte to the image of them as strikers and saboteurs, the men worked on to complete orders. Despite the support and admiration of the people of Glasgow, they were undermined by economics and the currents of history, leaving a slimmed-down, modernised shipyard industry and lasting rancour at Westminster betrayal.

Shipbuilding had been central to the consciousness of 1960s Glasgow. Cranes laced the horizon and formed the backdrop to our daily lives. In school holidays we were instructed to come home for dinner at the sound of the 'one o'clock horn', which signalled the end of the dinner break at the yards. In school we chanted 'Glasgow made the Clyde and the Clyde made Glasgow' and when the Queen launched Cunard's *Queen Elizabeth 2* in 1967 our whole school sat on the floor of the assembly hall and watched the event on a tiny, distant, black and white television. For decades, just before midnight on Hogmanay we would step outside to hear the ships' sirens herald in the new year. In 1985 we came out into the street and there was silence. There were no hooters; there were no ships.

13. The Winds of Change

Shipbuilding had provided work for lawyers, solicitors and insurance brokers, it had influenced the rail network, supply chains and university curricula. In the yards themselves thousands of men, and their sons and their sons' sons, were proud to master skills which were admired around the world. Working together in heavy industry, in tough physical conditions, fostered an ethos of common masculinity and mutual support, where men laboured and were proud of the fruits of their labour. And it was gone. There was less of an expectation that a son would follow his father into the factory or the yard, both from a lack of jobs there and from greater opportunities elsewhere. For older men, transition to other industries was difficult as they lacked the skills or desire to work in offices or service industries.

For over a century the identifiable enemy for many Glaswegians had been the Catholic Church – the whore of Babylon – and the Pope, the Antichrist. There were many Catholics in Glasgow, usually poor Irish immigrants who remained poor and educationally segregated. In the 1960s a prospective employer did not need to ask what religion a job applicant had – he just asked what school he or she had gone to, and if it had been St Aloysius or St Thomas Aquinas there was no law to stop them being rejected for that reason. Primary school children trilled, 'hail, hail the pope's in jail – give him a banana …'. But, as the missionary Eric Kirton had noticed when he returned from Malaysia, the world was changing. With the decline of the shipyards and steelworks came a loosening of tribal and sectarian bonds. In a world more focused on profit and loss than on maintaining communities, firms began to value candidates' aptitude for a post more than their religious affiliation.

The traditional male bastions were falling as women began to assert themselves. Young people, university-educated beneficiaries of their parents' wartime sacrifices, were beginning to question the established order. In the eyes of the new generation, prosperous as never before and rising up the social ladder thanks to free higher education, benefits and free healthcare, war was wrong, discipline crushed individualism, and the older generation, who had made enormous sacrifices to create this brave new world, were condemned for clinging stubbornly to outmoded ideas and for blocking progress. To a frisson of collective horror, John Lennon claimed that the Beatles were more popular than Jesus. Jack noted that you could listen to the BBC's *Thought for the Day* for weeks on end without hearing the word 'sin'.[1]

It was becoming more difficult to stay separate from the World. As the purists had feared, entertainment was the main threat, but it was television rather than the dreaded cinema which now beamed lust, foul language and rebellion into their homes. They saw women cavorting on *Top of the Pops* or becoming government ministers and company directors.[2] They saw young people in Paris,

---

1. This daily programme on BBC Radio 4 offered 'reflections from a faith perspective on issues and people in the news' – quote from *BBC – Religion and Ethics – Programmes*.
2. *Top of the Pops* was a weekly television show featuring that week's best-selling records, some performed by the original artists and some accompanied by Pan's People, a female dance troupe.

13. The Winds of Change

America and Grosvenor Square flouting authority and upsetting the carefully reconstructed post-war order, and it became increasingly difficult to steer young folk through a moral minefield which, in the absence of priests and creed, could only be negotiated with the guidance of one's own conscience and direct instructions from God.

Anniesland Hall had become relatively wealthy, confident and educated. The close-knit community of like-minded and mutually supportive Christians had been numerous and varied enough to be largely self-sufficient. The habits of bible study and self-discipline, ingrained since their infancy, had raised its members up through the social strata, and mutual trust encouraged Hall members to give their custom to small Brethren businesspeople, who in turn employed young Hall members as apprentices and older members as their lawyers and accountants. Now the Hall was opening up. Anniesland is close to Glasgow's universities, student halls of residence and nursing schools. It attracted a constant stream of educated young people who, through their studies and professions, were exposed to colleagues from different denominations who were, demonstrably, of equal professional or academic worth. As the Hall young folk mingled they recognised themselves – studious, fun-loving, concerned about poverty and disease throughout the world.

In his study of the educational attainments of Brethren children of manual workers, Ian Ford (himself a college teacher and member of nniesland Hall) demonstrated that they performed better than both non-Brethren children of manual workers, and middle-class children.³ This advantage was less marked when it came to university education, but nevertheless the proportion of Brethren boys at universities matched those of other denominations. Brethren girls were not so highly represented – while the ratio of British men and women entering university was 3:2, for Brethren women it was less than 5:1. This may have been due to Brethren concerns that universities encouraged students to question received wisdom, or to a feeling that a woman rendered service best at home, or to the perceived promiscuity and lack of discipline in 1960s universities.

The result of this further education was that, armed with their degrees and diplomas, Brethren young folk joined the professional classes. They increasingly held managerial or white-collar jobs, and through association and marriage with Christian students and doctors they became part of the Scottish educated bourgeoisie. Often, as is the case with educated working-class people, many became teachers, as well as doctors, lawyers and engineers. They were now less vulnerable to economic downturns than their working-class parents; they were more mobile, less fearful and less dependent on their tribe; they had not fought in uniform. In the safe and comfortable world that their parents had created for them they had the confidence to look outwards without fear. However, too much confidence ran perilously close to the sin of pride. When I rushed home from primary school to announce that I was top of the class and had been

---

3. Ford, 'Religious Affiliation and Achievement', pp. 20–24.

given a box shaped like a telephone kiosk filled with Cadbury's jazzies (chocolate drops covered in hundreds and thousands) I was ordered to stop boasting. But I had earned the jazzies and, so I wouldn't have to share, ate the lot that afternoon. I was sick. It was worth it.

The chaplains the young folk met at university promoted charities like Oxfam and Christian Aid, which had arisen as part of the new world order. Like Britain itself, the established churches were realising they could no longer dictate to the rest of the world, but had a duty to use their wealth and privilege to support the needy and press for social change. Time spent thinking about ways to improve society was time not spent on poring over the scriptures. As the young folk explored new ideas and broadened their minds, the World, created by God Himself, began to look like an opportunity rather than a threat.

The changes in the social composition of the Brethren presented a challenge and exposed Anniesland Hall to criticism from other assemblies. As Neil Dickson noted, 'assemblies of a predominantly working-class composition tended to remain conservative'.[4] Partly under the influence of American evangelicals, partly as a reaction to growing liberalism, some of the more working-class congregations became increasingly sectarian. For them, in this time of change, eternal truths provided a bulwark against uncertainty. Anniesland Hall was regarded by some as dangerously liberal. One young woman, marrying into Anniesland, was warned by her home assembly in Kilmarnock about 'dancing in the aisles' (whether

---

4. Dickson, p. 242.

literally or figuratively is not clear). The Kilmarnock reaction was symptomatic of the urban/rural divide, which was becoming more apparent in the Brethren and throughout society.

Some members of society in general were moving from the concept of discipline and punishment to that of understanding the causes of anti-social behaviour and providing support and rehabilitation. There was an increasing acknowledgement that reprehensible actions stemmed less from inherent evil and more from adverse life experiences. Many Hall people whose professions obliged them to consider various viewpoints, and to interact with humans in need of care, understanding and support, derived no satisfaction from haranguing or remaining apart from sinners. They saw flaws in Brethren practices and virtues in people of other denominations or none. As their view of the world widened, so did their perception of God, whose nature had been perceived for so long as that of a dominant male. If God was divine, surely He could not be constrained by the limits of human imagination.

Many members of Anniesland and other liberal Brethren meetings searched for a God who was indeed divine and transcendent, and for a faith which followed the spirit of Jesus' teachings, instead of selecting biblical verses to support entrenched views. Jesus' principal commandment was that we love our neighbours as ourselves, and to liberals, these neighbours were not necessarily evangelical Christians. The younger Christians felt that love encompasses caring, understanding and acceptance. For too long, love had been travestied as disciplinarian and didactic, a means to prevent the weak from straying rather than to nurture and encourage them to fulfil themselves, and to accept them as brothers and sisters. Thoughtful people searched in the scriptures, in their hearts and in other doctrines and faiths for a way to reconcile a fuller emulation of Christ with membership of the Brethren.

> Let the woman learn in silence with all subjection. But I suffer not a woman to teach, nor to usurp the authority over the man, but to be in silence.
> 1 Timothy 2:11-12

By the 1980s more women had been to university, more were working and, when the laws and childcare provision had improved, returned to work after having children. But the Brethren were still substantially male-dominated, which disheartened articulate, ambitious women. They began to press for a more active role, and some appeared at services with their heads uncovered. Elders marshalled the scriptures to demonstrate the ungodliness of allowing women to take a prominent role, but the argument began to look self-serving.

Across the Brethren, the rule of older males had become so irksome that large numbers of younger families were now leaving many assemblies to join the Baptist church, or to establish their own congregations. The reasons they gave were mainly 'the long sermons of speakers who do not always have the gift of preaching', narrowness in terms of thought and interaction with outside world, and the requirement that women remain silent.[5]

By 1968 there had been an Anniesland Hall in various forms for 100 years, but the centenary celebrations were overshadowed by the discovery that dry rot had set in. Surveyors were brought in to diagnose the extent of the damage and to prescribe a remedy, but despite numerous interventions, the rot continued to spread throughout the building.

By the 1980s it had reached the point where, without drastic action, the structure was in danger of collapse. In any case, by then the grandiose architecture of the Hall seemed inappropriate for a modern community. The antiquated toilets and huge, cold, white-tiled kitchens with their old-fashioned tea urns lacked the most basic modern appliances. When it was clear that the fabric of the building had become so riddled with dry rot that it was beyond repair, it was agreed that the Hall would be demolished and replaced by a less ostentatious and more practical suite of rooms occupying a smaller footprint. Much of the remaining land would be sold, creating a shopping mall where the original main entrance had been.

Lawyers in the congregation oversaw contracts, transfers of Trust moneys and the sale of valuable land. With the proceeds a new, comfortable, energy-efficient hall would be built on the remaining land. In 1989 the assembly members watched the wrecking balls reduce the mighty structure of the Hall to dust. This would be a new beginning.

But it was not.

---
5. Dickson, p. 348.

13. The Winds of Change

It was not just the building which was shattered. Not all the members of the Hall had gone to university, and not all had flourished in the post-war world. These Christians saw bare-headed women at the breaking of bread, even speaking and praying at services, wine served at dinner parties, and sermons that were less concerned with preaching to the ungodly than with sharing insights from spiritual experiences. They saw people from different denominations invited to speak at meetings, and co-operation with non-Brethren groups. They saw confident, even arrogant, younger people who did not hesitate to criticise their elders. Anniesland was not a sanctuary from the World, it was contaminated by it. What these people were unable to see was a longing to change the Hall from within. The liberals rejoiced that they had found the love of Christ, and yearned to serve the Lord by steering the Hall in an inclusive, socially aware direction.

The young people had learnt well from meditative preachers like George Harpur and from theologians like Dietrich Bonhoeffer, who argued that Christians should not retreat from the world but act within it. Younger men (in their forties) who had hoped to be included as elders, and steer the Hall towards compassionate, socially active witness, found no encouragement. They tried to innovate within the Hall itself. Once a month, after the breaking of bread, hall members gathered for a soup and cheese lunch – rolls, cheese and home-made tomato soup – which served two purposes: the nominal fee went towards missionary work; and the event itself was an occasion for fellowship. The new generation saw service to the unsaved as service to the Lord, but some elders pointed out that when Jesus praised those who visited the sick and gave drink to the thirsty, these good deeds were done to 'the least of my brethren' – the Brethren, not the unsaved. Yet the more the elders dug in, the more quietly determined were the younger members to serve God in the way they understood it, in their hearts and by their actions.

The elders themselves had long been divided on the fundamental tenets of the Hall. For traditionalists, the new questioning of accepted practice was a breach of discipline and respect, as well as an existential threat to the souls of the rebels and to the integrity of the Hall itself. It was not for nothing that people who left the Brethren were known as 'backsliders'. Anyone who did not subscribe absolutely to the accepted truths had embarked on a slippery slope, and 'watered-down' Christianity was diluted with self-indulgence and sin. Jack and other less confident men, who revered authority and lacked the intellectual self-confidence to allow their beliefs to evolve, or to enter into a reasoned argument with what were now their opponents, saw the Hall veering off course. Without the cast-iron truths of the Gospel they would be cast adrift, at the mercy of any persuasive, indeed seductive, argument and would lose hold of Jesus' hand.[6] The

---

6. Matthew 14:29-31. 'And he [Jesus, who was walking on the sea of Galilee] said, Come. And when Peter was come down out of the ship, he walked on the water, to go to Jesus. But when he saw the wind boisterous, he was afraid; and beginning to sink, he cried, saying, Lord, save me. And immediately Jesus stretched forth his hand, and caught him, and said unto him, O thou of little faith, wherefore didst thou doubt?'

harder the liberals tugged in one direction, the more tenaciously the traditionalists pulled back.

As is so often the case, the traditionalists sought to hold back the tide by tightening their control. These had been the tactics of the Haldanes many years before, but even with his power and money Haldane had eventually been left behind, and this was beginning to be the case in Anniesland.

As happens with many schisms, of the many complex causes, one identifiable breaking point was the single, irrational issue of hats. For female doctors, lawyers and head teachers the insistence on dictating a woman's choice of clothing represented an attempt by older men to subordinate them; for the traditionalists, the women's choice was an outward sign of rebellion against God. The liberals saw this as an imposition of appearance over intent – even as far back as the time of the prophets, God had reminded Samuel that 'man looketh on the outward appearance, but the Lord looketh on the heart'.[7] They had, after all, witnessed strident evangelists fulminating against sin while themselves committing adultery, and seen their own male elders and fellow Christians preaching love but raging against insubordination. They longed for participative consensus, but came up against authoritarians. As so often when ideologies clash, common ground shrank to nothing.

After several years of discussion, the schism had become too bitter and the brightest and best indicated that the best solution would be for them to leave. One Thursday evening in 1989 the Annual General

---

7. 1 Samuel 16:7

Meeting (the only occasion women were allowed to speak) was convened. A young woman with a prize in logic from Glasgow University delivered a carefully prepared explanation of the liberals' position, which was greeted by heckling – 'and that's why we don't let women speak!' The traditionalists saw that it was time to stand and fight. That weekend they sent out a letter of ultimatum. At a soup and cheese lunch on the Sunday, the liberals decided they had no choice but to go. One of them, who worked in the education department, arranged for a school hall to be available for their use, from that same evening. Out of 120 families, 70 left.

Their decision was not taken lightly. Even people who were eminent in trade and the professions felt their core identity was as members of the Hall. They had grown up in the Hall, calling Hall members who were not blood relatives, aunties and uncles. They had been married there, and brought up their children within the Hall, where they were nurtured and mentored by the community. They recalled Santa at Sunday School Christmas parties, the togetherness of the Sail, skiing in the Scottish highlands and hill-walking. Those who had experienced hardship or bereavement had not borne their troubles alone, but had been able to rely on the Hall's generous practical and emotional support. Many were faced with agonising choices: whether to stay and attempt to reform the Hall from within, or to leave parents behind; or to keep their children in the Hall, although the vast majority of the young people had gone. Friends were divided. Couples might have different views yet had to agree a

13. The Winds of Change

joint course of action. One woman, thirty years later, sighed, 'I still don't know what happened.'

The bright new hall took shape the following year. It was elegant and spacious, incorporating some of the most finely crafted features of the old building. There were pink carpets in the sunlit meeting rooms and brightly coloured toys in a side hall for the toddler groups. The toilets were modern and easy to clean (and flush). The old tea urns were replaced by electric kettles and microwaves. After coffee mornings, instead of vainly searching in the cold for dry dish towels the ladies could relax and chat while the dishwasher hummed. Outside groups asked to use the rooms for their mother and toddler groups and small clubs. This was a chance for the Hall to play a central role in the community, but instead they turned inward.

Like the original Brethren, the secessionists wanted no material assets or grand buildings. They formed West Glasgow New Church, a loose association of like-minded Christians who rented old church halls and school halls for their meetings.

As the Brethren continued to evolve into a wider, more upwardly mobile movement, the congregations in more working class districts aged, dwindled and eventually closed their doors. Anniesland Hall took the remaining congregants from these assemblies into its bosom, rejoicing in the increased numbers and wider range of personalities.

After the initial warm welcome the incomers took stock of their new world and measured it against their interpretation of the scriptures. In comparison with the incomers, even the remaining members of the Hall had been slightly shifted by the tide of liberalism. The move towards didacticism and the increased preponderance of older people weighed on members who had not left in the original schism. They stayed for a while, then, as the numbers of young people shrank further, moved with their children to St George's Tron, an evangelical Church of Scotland establishment.

They endured further controversy at the Tron. In 2011 the General Assembly of the Church of Scotland decided to accept gay ministers, provided they had declared their sexuality and were ordained before 2009. In 2013 the General Assembly voted to allow congregations to admit gay ministers, but only if each individual congregation decided to do so. In 2012, feeling that the Church of Scotland had 'chosen to walk away from the biblical gospel, and to walk apart from the faith of the worldwide Christian Church', 500 members of the Tron left the Kirk entirely. The Church, for its part, claimed that the secessionists owed it almost £1 million and sent the Sheriff's officers to recover church property.

After bitter wrangling over several years, the Anniesland Christians endeavoured to remain on good terms and continued to meet in other venues as friends and fellow-Christians. When Jack died, his funeral in Maryhill was attended by folks from across the divide. As the crowd watched his coffin being lowered into the grave he would share with his stillborn grandson, a man in a black leather jacket and shades, a recent arrival to Anniesland Hall from the now defunct assemblies, stepped forward and delivered a 'pit-dangling' call to repentance.[8] Perhaps he was fulfilling a long-held vow to repay Jack's kindness to him; perhaps seeing some of Jack's non-Brethren relatives weeping at the sight of the baby's headstone, he felt God had called him to exhort the unsaved to seize this opportunity to break the chains of sin. The winds swept down from the Campsies and the clouds darkened, but still he declaimed.

Nessie silently clutched her granddaughter's hand; meek and courageous as ever, she said nothing, but the next day instructed her lawyer that there would be no graveside speech at her funeral.

---

8. Figuratively dangling souls over the fiery pit of hell, 'where their worm dieth not, and the fire is not quenched' (Mark 9.48).

Postscript

In some respects, the story of Anniesland Hall is the story of Glasgow and indeed, of Great Britain. Its wealth was founded on a spirit of adventure, courage and vision, but also on wilful blindness. The Oswalds sought new worlds to conquer, confident that the entire world was a golden opportunity. Heirs of the Enlightenment, they believed in change and progress. However, even as the Oswalds were following their dreams of wealth and influence, their contemporaries were beginning to question the basis on which this wealth was built. Richard of Auchincruive, one of the most successful Glasgow slave traders, was personally acquainted with, and indeed a friend of, people who were fundamentally opposed to slavery and who would have made their point of view clear in discussions with him, but this seems to have left him cold.

The link between the wealth of the Oswalds and Anniesland Hall was the Haldane family, who had the self-belief of many in nineteenth-century Britain. They, like the Brethren, were open to new ways of spreading God's Word; they were less open to other interpretations of that Word and less inclined to tolerate resistance. By the time the Haldanes had restyled themselves the Gordon Oswalds they were, like Great Britain itself, less swashbuckling than their antecedents and keener on building a solid world. They were still certain that they knew what a solid and decent world looked like. This was the world into which the Brethren were born, a world in which right-thinking men and women had control of their lives, and indeed their eternal lives. Custodians of the truth, they had a duty to bring others to that truth, and to cast dissenters out.

By the later twentieth century Western hegemony was faltering. Great Britain had become a second-tier power and Glasgow had fallen into steep decline. Seeing the failures of the didacticism of communism, thoughtful Westerners began to question the validity of their own previous assumptions of the superiority of their rigid systems and ideas, and to see value in other beliefs. For the Brethren, this began with appreciating the beliefs and practices of other Christians, and spread to an interest in other faiths and to valuing personal spirituality over campaigning proselytising.

Anniesland Hall was no exception to this growing respect for other beliefs, nor to its corollary, reaction. In Glasgow, as in Anniesland Hall, attempts to hold back the tide meant that the damage – to trades union members as well as to worshippers – was greater than it would have been had the people who were affected embraced change and worked together to find new ways to prosper in an altered world. Those with education and confidence seized the new opportunities, as had Oswald centuries before, and flourished; those who did not became increasingly impotent, inward-looking and bitter. This is the story of communities and generations since time began. In a spirit of humility and acceptance of potential loss of power, the wise have endeavoured to discern which changes are for the better, and which should be resisted in order to preserve essential values.

The 2020 Covid-19 epidemic was the final nail in the coffin of Anniesland Hall. The focal point of worship, the Breaking of Bread, was suspended for longer than in many assemblies who, to prevent infection, had changed from drinking wine from a common cup to using separate vessels. After much prayerful discussion the elders decided that all biblical references (e.g. 1 Corinthians 11:26: 'For as often as ye eat this bread and drink this cup') were to a *single* cup. As by this time the average age of members was over seventy-five, sharing a cup could not be countenanced by most of them on health grounds, so they did not partake. The spiritual and emotional costs of this were profound. The Hall itself is as well-appointed as ever, but dwarfs the dwindling congregation. The Hall now seems to mirror Anniesland Cross, which is as windswept as ever, and like many contemporary British high streets, is strangely desolate. Gone are the florists, banks, dress shops and tea shops and in their place are lower-rank supermarkets and charity shops. West Glasgow New Church, by contrast, is thriving, a place of joy, fellowship, lively discussion and social commitment. The Anniesland Hall elders are aware that their community is dying out, and are sharing the premises with Christ Church. They currently have no intention of bequeathing their property to their prodigal sons, and like James William Gordon Oswald before them, are assessing deserving beneficiaries. Exclusion from this material inheritance does not weigh heavily on the folk at West Glasgow New Church. Yet for some, on both sides of the divide, the sense of loss – of childhood friends, of the security of a loving community and of the old certainties – remains a deep, nagging ache.

Acknowledgements

This book would never have been completed without the support of many friends:
- Huge thanks to Terry Turner who read the manuscript in several forms and offered constructive advice and encouragement
- Also Harry Potter, who proofread the manuscript and offered practical advice
- And many friends in Glasgow who corrected my misappprehensions and provided practical information
- Chris Moore gave me useful thoughts on the manuscript
- Ian Mackay kindly copied original documents from the Anniesland Hall archive
- Anthea Church advised me on publishing, and recommended my excellent publisher, Alison Shakspeare
- Andy, my husband, drove me around Scotland so I could carry out research
- The wardens at Auchincruive Church provided me with valuable information
- And Rose insisted that I should not leave the manuscript unpublished, as I owe it to all my

dear friends to let them see what they helped me achieve.

I am responsible for any factual inaccuracies. The recollections are mine and, to coin a phrase, recollections may vary.

Bibliography

Allan, John, 'The Local Church and Evangelism', *The Harvester*, LIX: 1 (January 1979) pp. 16–20

Anniesland Hall, 'History of A Hall', privately produced leaflet.

Beattie, David, *Brethren: The story of a great recovery* (Kilmarnock, 1940)

Breen, Timothy H., *Tobacco Culture: The Mentality of the Great Tidewater Planters on the Eve of Revolution* (Princeton, 1985)

Butterfield, L.H. (ed.), Diary and Autobiography of John Adams, (Cambridge, Mass, 1961).

Dickson, Neil, *Brethren in Scotland: A Social Study of an Evangelical Movement* (Milton Keynes, 2002)

Donald, Colin, *Minute Book of the Board of Green Cloth 1809–1820 With notices of the Members* (Glasgow, 1891)

Edinburgh University Library Special Collections (EULSC), GB237, Coll 521

Ford, Ian, 'Religious Affiliation and Achievement: a note on the "Brethren" in western Scotland', *Scottish Educational Studies*, 3: 1 (May 1971)

Hague, William, *William Wilberforce: The Life of the Great Anti-Slave Trade Campaigner* (London 2007)

Haldane, Alexander, *Memoirs of the Lives of Robert Haldane of Airthrey and of his Brother, James Alexander Haldane* (London, 1852)

Haldane, Richard Burdon, *Richard Burdon Haldane: An Autobiography* (London, 1929)

Hancock, David, *Citizens of the World: London Merchants and the Integration of the British Atlantic Community, 173 –1785* (Cambridge, 1995)

Harpur, George, *Meet the Book* (London, 1962)

Hays, Mary, *Memoirs of Emma Courtney* (London, 2000)

MacCulloch, Diarmaid, *Reformation: Europe's House Divided 1490–1700* (London, 2004)

Mackie, J.D., B. Lenman and G. Parker, A History of Scotland (London, 1991)

Martin, David, *Auchincruive: the History of the West of Scotland Agricultural College*, (Ayrshire, 1994)

McUre, John, The History of Glasgow. A View of the City of Glasgow: or, an account of its origin, rise and progress (Glasgow 1830)

Morris, Richard B., *The Peacemakers: The Great Powers and American Independence* (London 1965)

Moss, Michael and Iain Russell, *Range and Vision: the First Hundred Years of Barr & Stroud* (Glasgow 1988)

Namier, L. and J. Brooke (eds), *The History of Parliament: the House of Commons 1754–1790*, (1964)

O'Byrne, Robert, *Left Without a Handkerchief* (Dublin, 2022)

Parker, Matthew, *The Sugar Barons: Family, Corruption, Empire and War* (London, 2012)

Peters, Carolyn Marie, 'Glasgow's Tobacco Lords: An Examination of Wealth Creators in the Eighteenth Century' (PhD thesis, University of Glasgow, 1990).

Reid, Robert and James Pagan, *Glasgow Past and Present* (Glasgow, 1884)

Thomas, David A., *Malta Convoys* (Barnsley, 1999)

Urquhart, Gordon R., *Along Great Western Road: An Illustrated History of Glasgow's West End* (Mauchline, 2000)

Family Trees

Oswald family tree 220
Talbot Crosbie family tree 221
Alexander Oswald family tree 222
Haldane family tree 223

Greyed-out boxes indicate line of inheritance

Blood of the Lamb

Oswald family tree

- James Oswald of Kirkwall c. 1590-1660
  - Barbara
  - Rev. James 1654-1698 (Episcopelian)
    - Richard 1687-1766
    - Alexander 1694-1763
  - Rev. George (Presbyterian) 1674 -
    - Elizabeth
    - George
    - Rev. James 1703-1793 (Moderator)
    - Richard of Auchincruive 1705-1784 m. Mary 1719-1788
      - ? Anderson m Alexander / Christian O. / John
      - Alexander O. of Shieldhall 1738-1813 married Margaret Dundas
        - Richard Alexander O. of Moore Park (-1821)
        - James O. 1779-1853 (MP)
          - Alexander Haldane O. 1811-1868 MP
            - 2 daughters + James Haldane O. 1848-1866
          - George O. of Auchincruive 1813-1871
            - Major Julian O. 1860-1943
              - George O.
                - Admiral of the Fleet Sir John Julian Robertson O. 1933-2011
            - Richard Alexander O. 1841-1921
      - George O. of Scotstoun and Auchincruive 1735-1819
        - Elizabeth 1767-1864
        - Catherine (-1843)
          - Christian m. Alexander Anderson
        - Robert Haldane (-1842)
        - James 1774-1822
        - Margaret 1787-1849 m. James Farquhar Gordon (1772-1843)
          - James Farquhar Gordon O. 1818-1897 m. 1844 Thomazine Crawford c. 1816-1881
            - Emma Anne Talbot Crosbie 1851-1897 m. 1885
            - James William Gordon O. 1854-1937 m. 1878 Eugenie Diane Coke 1854-1947
              - Lt Col. Adrian Gordon Paterson DSO (1888-1940)
                - Richard drowned 1939
        - Louisa 1772-1798 m Richard Alexander of Auchincruive MP 1771-1841
          - Mary 1780-1851 m Lilias 1773-1845
          - Richard 1797-1834 m. Lady Mary Kennedy 1799-1886
          - Margaret Hester 1794-1855

220

Family Trees

Talbot Crosbie family tree

```
Rev. John Talbot Crosbie d.1818
    │
    ├── William Talbot Crosbie 1817-1899
    │       │
    │       ├── Emma Anne Talbot Crosbie 1850-1897 —m. 1885— James Farquhar Gordon Oswald 1818-1897 —m— Thomasine Crawford c.1816-1881
    │       │                                                          │
    │       │                                                   James William Gordon Oswald 1854-1937
    │       │                                                          │
    │       │                                                         m. 1878
    │       │                                                          │
    │       │                                                   Eugenie Diana Coke 1854-1947
    │       │
    │       └── Lyndsey Talbot Crosbie 1844-1913 —m— Anne Crosbie Coke
    │
    └── Diana Talbot Crosbie c.1816-1895 —m— Col. Edward Thomas Coke 1807-1888
```

221

Blood of the Lamb

Alexander Oswald family tree

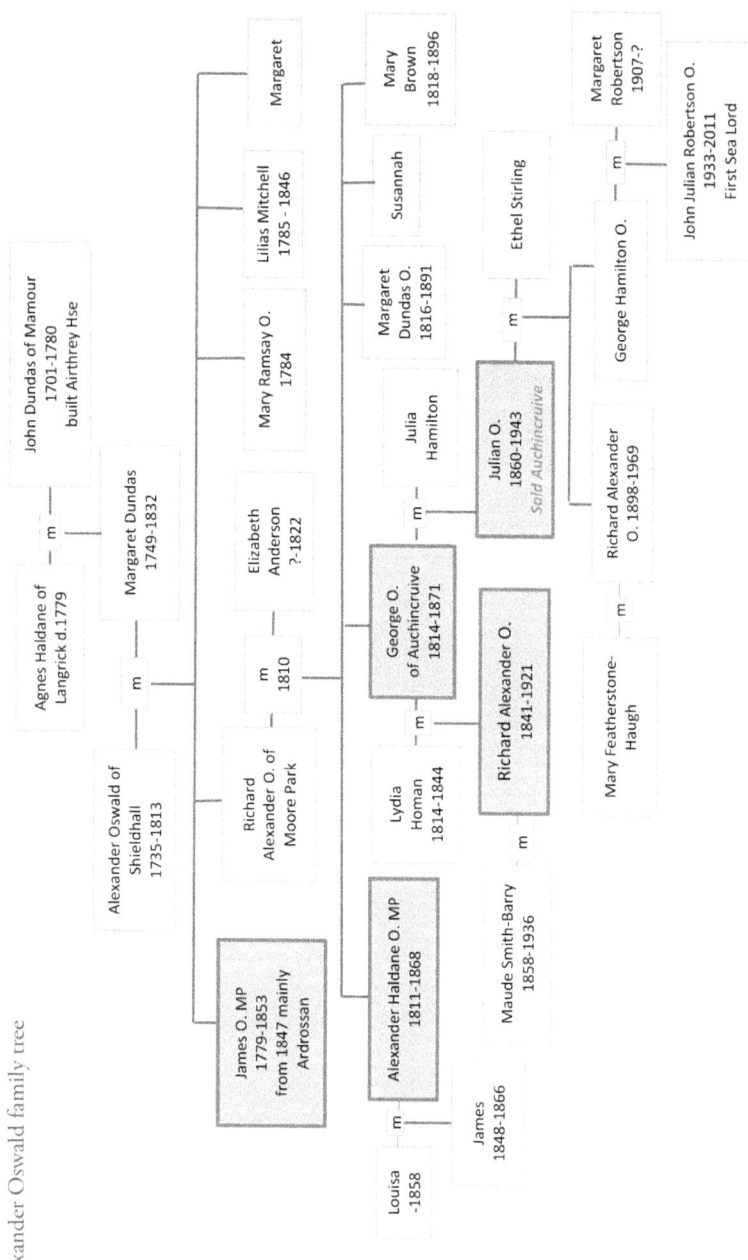

Family Trees

Haldane family tree

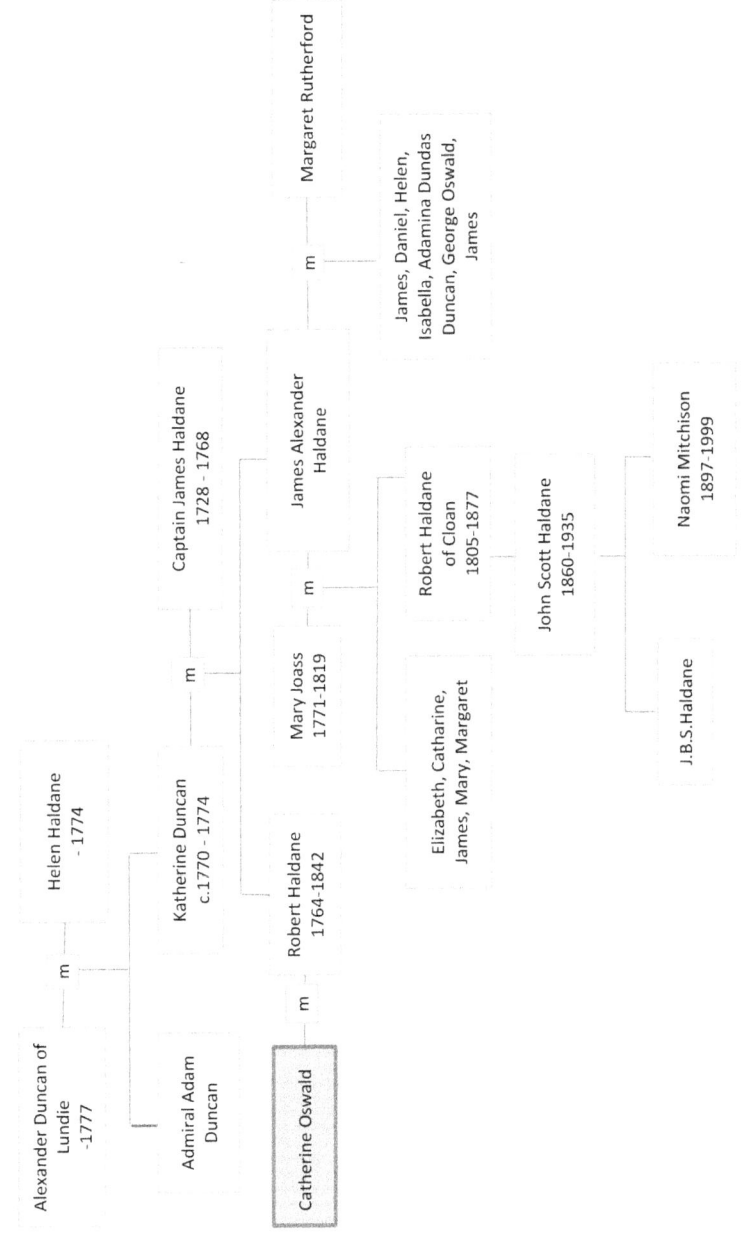

Index

A

Adam, Robert 72
Adams, John 42, 46
Airthrey estate 69, 72, 75, 77, 83, 122
American Independence 30, 38
Anniesland Cross 129, 171, 212
Anniesland Hall 2, 3, 7, 20, 23, 47–48, 56, 60, 68, 73, 78, 82, 92, 95, 101, 106, 109, 110–111, 112, 114, 117, 120, 125, 148–150, 154, 159, 162–163, 165, 167, 172, 182, 197, 199, 202, 207–208, 210–212
Anniesland Mansions 95, 112, 114, 146, 170
Auchincruive church. *See* St. Quivox

B

Barr & Stroud 129, 130, 131, 132, 138, 139
Beggs, John (Jonny) 126, 127
Beggs, Rebecca (Ruby) 127
Birss, Alec 172
Blessit, Arthur 180
Bogue, Dr David 73, 74
Breconshire, MV (HMS?) 118, 119, 133

Brethren 3, 15, 78, 99–111, 117, 125, 132–133, 136, 150–151, 157, 161, 162, 165–166, 173, 179, 182, 184, 197–209, 210–211
Brethren, Close 166
Brethren, Plymouth 3, 7, 64, 65, 95, 100, 108, 141, 142, 146, 151, 162, 165, 166
British and Foreign Bible Society 74–75, 80
Bunce Island 29, 36–37
Burns, Robert 44–46, 52–54

C

Cochrane, Andrew 16, 21
Coke, Eugenie Diana (later Oswald) 95, 110
Congregational Church 66–67, 73, 77–78, 91, 108
Cunninghame, William, the elder 23, 38, 65
Cunninghame, William, the younger 65–67, 80

D

Darby, John Nelson 65, 100, 101
Drumchapel 123, 158, 170–172
Duncan, Admiral Adam 70–71

F

Ferguson, Pastor Malcolm 116–117, 125
Ferguson, Sir Alex 167
Florida 30–31, 38

Ford, Barbara 99, 113
Ford, Ian 197
Forth and Clyde canal 47, 48, 84
Franklin, Benjamin 26, 40–42

G

Gibraltar, seige of 41
Gilbert Scott, George 89–90
Glasgow United Evangelistic Association (GUEA) 110, 116–117, 161
Glasgow University 9, 19, 52, 90, 128, 130, 206
Graham, Billy 177–178
Grangemouth 140–143, 146
Great Western Road 23, 88–90, 95, 108, 110–111, 112–115, 122, 146, 171, 173, 190

H

Haldane, James Alexander 60, 73–78
Haldane, Robert 33, 42, 60, 69–83
Harpur, George 160–161, 203
Hayman, David 182–183

J

Jackson, Annie 124–125, 135
Jackson, Jack (Jackie) 1, 115, 117, 121–146, 164–170, 172–175, 178–180, 183, 208–209
Jackson, Mary 125–126, 146
Jackson, May 124, 126

Jackson, Nessie 140–146, 150, 164–167, 172, 175, 178–179, 209
Jackson, Rebecca 121, 124
Jackson, Rena 124
Jackson, William (Bill) 135, 155, 178
Jackson, William (Willie) 122, 125–126, 137–138
Jamaica 13, 26, 30, 46, 54
Jay, John 40, 42
Jordanhill 52, 84–85, 88, 92, 140, 144
Jordanhill College 167

K

Kirton, Eric 162–163, 195
Knightswood 68, 108–109, 122–124
Knox, John 63

L

Laurens, Henry 26, 30, 42–43
Laurens, John 35
Leitch, Charles Alexander 141–147
Leitch, Ina (Jemima McKee) 141–146

M

Matheson, Duncan 109
McLean, Donald 115, 125, 128, 149
McNair, Lachlan 115, 117–119, 125
McNair report 139–140
Mining 68, 90, 141
Missionaries 74, 77, 115, 156, 161–164, 167, 203

Mitchison, Naomi 60
Moody, Dwight L. 107–108

N
New Lanark 90–91

O
Oswald family 7, 50–68, 84–95
Alexander 8, 11, 16, 21, 24
Alexander Haldane 57–59
Alexander of Shieldhall 35
Catherine Haldane 68, 71–72
Elizabeth 67–68
Eugenie. See Coke, Eugenie Diana
George of Scotstoun and Auchincruive 19, 50–52, 71
James Farquhar Gordon 68
James, MP 55–57
James William Gordon 7
Lilias 53–54, 83
Lucy (Louisa) 52–53
Margaret 53, 58, 72
Richard 8, 10, 16–17, 21, 24
Richard Alexander of Auchincruive 52–54
Richard Alexander of Moore Park 55
Richard of Auchincruive 13–15, 24, 25–48

P
Partick, Glasgow Borough of 92, 121, 167, 172
Plymouth Brethren. *See* Brethren, Plymouth

Port Sunlight 91

Q
Quakers 34, 104

R
Ramsay, Mary 26–27
Reformation 19, 34, 61–68

S
Sankey, Ira D. 107–108
Schools
  Barrowfield 167–169
  Broomhill 170
  Church Street 167–169
  Glasgow Academy 155
Scotstoun 23–24, 50–60, 67–68, 83, 84–95, 122
Scottish Counties Evangelistic Movement (SCEM) 179
Shelburne, Lord, Prime Minister 40–43
Shipbuilding 194–195
Sin 2, 23, 64, 66, 82, 99, 105–106, 114, 116, 126, 152, 174, 177, 181, 189–191, 196, 198, 204, 205, 209
Sinclair, Evelyn 184–191
Smith, Archibald 52
Society for the Propagation of the Gospel at Home (SPGH) 77
South Carolina 30
Stephen, Clarice 186
Stephen, Duncan 172, 186
St George's Tron 208
St Mary's Cathedral 90, 190
Stores system 11–12, 37
St. Quivox 47, 53

Stuart, Mary, Queen of Scots 63
Stuart, Prince Charles Edward (Bonnie Prince Charlie) 15–17
St Vincent, Lord, John Jervis 70–71

T

Talbot Crosbie, Lyndsey 94–95, 110
Talbot Crosbie, William 94
Temple 122, 172–174, 184, 188
Thompson, Alexander 'Greek' 89
Thompson, Elizabeth 167, 170
Tobacco Lords 7–24, 37–38, 44, 65
Tontine Society 20–21
Trinity, The 150, 152

V

Victoria Park, Glasgow 83, 92, 132, 157
Virginia 11–13, 28, 37–39

W

Walker, Gary (Archie) 132, 173, 183
Wars
 Austrian Succession 27
 First World War 122, 130, 193
 Russo-Japanese 129
 Second World War 104, 106, 118, 134, 139, 143, 170
 Seven Years' War 27–28

Washington, George 38
Wilberforce, William 34, 37, 75–76, 81

www.ingramcontent.com/pod-product-compliance
Lightning Source LLC
Chambersburg PA
CBHW051556010526
44118CB00022B/2727